GW00659098

# Advance Praise

'The book uses true workplace stories to help professionals overcome four debilitating emotions—fear, sorrow, anger and disgust—and leverage the more positive emotions of love, courage, wonder and humour to achieve what we all yearn for as we strive for excellence in performance.'

**Ronnie Screwvala,** *Entrepreneur, Philanthropist and Author*

'We live in a world fraught with anger, stress, hatred and divisiveness. This spills from our society into our work and personal lives, and nothing in our upbringing has really prepared us to deal with these emotions. This book, using arts theory, which is centuries old, modern psychology and management practice, is a refreshing approach to diffusing these difficult situations and being able to deal with essential emotions that could [affect] our happiness and [keep us from achieving] self-fulfilment. I am sure it will help individuals and organizations.'

**Mallika Sarabhai,** *Classical Dancer, Choreographer and Activist*

# THE BUSINESS OF MANAGING EMOTIONS

# THE BUSINESS OF
# MANAGING
# EMOTIONS

## A Three-dimensional Approach

## MANJIRI GOKHALE JOSHI
## AND
## MANJEET SINGH

Los Angeles | London | New Delhi
Singapore | Washington DC | Melbourne

*First published in 2018 by*

**SAGE Publications India Pvt Ltd**
B1/I-1 Mohan Cooperative Industrial Area
Mathura Road, New Delhi 110 044, India
*www.sagepub.in*

**SAGE Publications Inc**
2455 Teller Road
Thousand Oaks, California 91320, USA

**SAGE Publications Ltd**
1 Oliver's Yard, 55 City Road
London EC1Y 1SP, United Kingdom

**SAGE Publications Asia-Pacific Pte Ltd**
3 Church Street
#10-04 Samsung Hub
Singapore 049483

Published by Vivek Mehra for SAGE Publications India Pvt Ltd, typeset in 11/14.5 pts Sabon by Fidus Design Pvt. Ltd., Chandigarh and printed at Chaman Enterprises, New Delhi.

Library of Congress Cataloging-in-Publication Data Available

**ISBN:** 978-93-528-0798-7 (PB)

**SAGE Team:** Manisha Mathews, Sandhya Gola, Megha Dabral and Rajinder Kaur

*To our erstwhile work selves who sometimes lost the battle to*

- *'anger' and quit when it was too early,*
- *festering 'disgust' that overstayed,*
- *unfounded 'fear' that led to failure and*
- *human-created 'sorrow' that touched our core;*

*and to our future work selves who hope to leverage*

- *'courage' to overcome the impediments,*
- *'humour' to spread joy,*
- *platonic 'love' to create 'wondrous' value;*

*and strive for the state of 'peace' that we all yearn to achieve at the workplace.*

Thank you for choosing a SAGE product!
If you have any comment, observation or feedback,
I would like to personally hear from you.

*Please write to me at* **contactceo@sagepub.in**

**Vivek Mehra,** Managing Director and CEO, SAGE India.

## Bulk Sales

SAGE India offers special discounts
for purchase of books in bulk.
We also make available special imprints
and excerpts from our books on demand.

*For orders and enquiries, write to us at*

Marketing Department
SAGE Publications India Pvt Ltd
B1/I-1, Mohan Cooperative Industrial Area
Mathura Road, Post Bag 7
New Delhi 110044, India

*E-mail us at* **marketing@sagepub.in**

## Subscribe to our mailing list
*Write to* **marketing@sagepub.in**

This book is also available as an e-book.

# Contents

# Detailed Contents

# List of Illustrations

## Tables

## Figures

# Preface

> *I don't want to be at the mercy of my emotions. I want to*
> *use them, to enjoy them, and to dominate them.*
>
> —Oscar Wilde, *The Picture of Dorian Gray*

Why do we work?

- To make money to take care of our basic needs?
- To make enough money so that one day we need not think about making money?
- To make the most of the time we have, to make ourselves feel good (for the fortunate few who are at a stage where they do not need to think about making money)?
- To be able to influence people, change lives for the better?

Picking from Maslow's[1] famous pyramid, we work for one of the following depending on the stage we are in life: for food, sustenance, self-esteem, love, belonging or self-actualization.

All of these reasons could be summarized as a single reason for work—to create value for others and ourselves.

And during this journey to create value, we 'feel'. Whether we are 'allowed to' demonstrate it in public or not and whether we 'admit' it to ourselves or not, whatever occurs at the workplace generates emotional moods.

---

[1] A.H. Maslow, 'A Theory of Human Motivation'. *Psychological Review* 50(1943): 370–96.

The emotional moods that are generated in us by the situations created at the workplace drive our decisions and behaviours that result in changing or not changing lives.

This book is an attempt to delve into these emotional moods, adopting a three-pronged approach—using the ancient *Navarasa*[2] theory of the Indian performing arts, the medical science behind emotions and the evolving social science of management. We have termed this confluence of the three lines of thought as the 3-DEM framework.

At the workplace, to what extent one shows one's emotions and how much importance one gives to building and nurturing relationships depend greatly on the social and cultural norms of various countries, regions, industries and the personal preferences of people themselves. But the truth is that these emotions exist, whether you give them a chance to matter or not.

This book has been written by two authors who met in a professional setting 12 years ago. Over the years, our subsequent diverse paths led us to experience the extreme highs and extreme lows of professional life. And unlike so many people who manage to sift the personal from the professional and keep 'operating without getting emotion in the way', there were times we could not. When the joys generated by our professional lives bubbled over into our individual personal spaces, they were welcome. But when the fear, sorrow, anger and disgust generated by workspaces hit, we were shaken. This book, in a way, is a long note to our former

---

[2] The *Navarasa* theory is mentioned in *The Natyashastra*—a treatise on dramatic 'theory' written in Sanskrit by Bharata Muni between 200 BC and 200 AD. See, Bharata Muni, *The Natyashastra*, trans. Manomohan Ghosh (Kolkata: Asiatic Society of Bengal, 1951).

selves, the ones who could not 'manage emotions' and let them impact our core.

So, in Manjeet's words, the genesis of the book:

June 2015, London: I was waiting near my office to meet Manjiri after almost a year. A lot had happened in that year. We met in Chiswick at The Old Pack Horse pub.

The last time I had met her, I was in a different space playing a different game. At that time, I had just taken up a dream job with an awesome salary in the City of London, a beautiful home, and had recently become a dad with a handsome boy who was just 3 weeks old. Walking into the office every day was inspiring. To see everyone suited up with their earphones on, some leafing through books as they stood in a queue and then disappearing into the tall building that was home to some of the biggest banks in the world.

The place buzzed till 9 AM and then suddenly everything went quiet until about noon when the 'executives' came out again to have their lunch. It was just another day for me but for the way I walked out of office on that Friday. I had quit just like that. Walked out frustrated, angry, irritated with everything and how it was not right, fair and justified. It did not take much—just a few people to trigger the moment when nothing mattered. At that moment, it did not even seem to matter that there was a few month-old baby at home and a family that depended on me.

As is generally the case, when Manjiri and I meet, I speak for the first 45 minutes pouring out all that has happened since we last met. And then, I smile having delved into my professional wins and woes asking her what she thinks I should do next.

On that day in early June, Manjiri was not surprised by what had happened to me a year ago. What surprised her the most was that I did not call anyone or her when

I made that decision. I was zoned out and, what I now see, undergoing an emotional Tsunami. One emotion took over everything. I knew how to play the game, I had played it before. I meet and coach so many entrepreneurs, senior executives who put up a poker face in front of the world while at workplace. And in a one-on-one coaching session they open up about their biggest desires to succeed at the workplace that are usually linked to their deepest feelings. But when I really should have been in control, my own feelings defeated me.

My experience in training and coaching failed me in my own game.

What had happened? Why did I quit? Why did my emotions play up? Who was to blame for what happened?

Now when I look back three years later, having picked up my professional life where I dropped it off for a few months and especially having completed the journey of writing this book, I realized there is no one to blame, not even me. I thought I had an emotional blackout, but that wasn't the case. Extreme happiness about getting the job I wasn't expecting coupled with the extreme stress of managing expectations caused an emotional wave I did not know how to respond to. I also realized how broken our education system is, which teaches us about subjects such as science and commerce, but it does not teach us to proactively explore how we feel and harness our emotions. I am now convinced that the power to pause and explore our feelings needs a structured exercise and training and this should be taught to everyone.

This book is a toolkit that will help explore the answer to the role emotions play at the workplace. It's a journey to understand why we cannot park emotions outside the office building and how we can channelize our emotions to become high achievers at work.

People are made redundant at short notice, including even those who have served organizations for many years. The golden sentence that seems to be the escape key to everything, 'Nothing personal, it is just business', is repeated and the person at the receiving end is expected to put up a brave face and move on.

You could be the CEO or have a leadership role in the company with the desire and goal to help your team to do and be more.

You could be an employee at the workplace who feels coming to work is an absolute drag and you really want to start enjoying work.

No role, job title, industry lacks emotion. If there are human beings, there will be emotions.

There are some chapters with powerful questions at the end. They help you clear and rewire your mind. The book has stories of people who dealt with emotions at the workplace in their unique ways. Use this book to reflect on whenever you feel or remember feeling a specific emotion in the past. Go to the chapter on that emotion and pick up one tool or answer some questions. And then reflect some more! Welcome to the journey of emotions at workplace!

# Acknowledgements

This book has been possible due to the support from the following people:

1. Abhay Joshi
2. Dr Bent Flyvbjerg
3. Elise Behr
4. Gauri Gokhale
5. Harpreet Kaur Kalsi
6. Madan Gokhale
7. Mahi Joshi
8. Manisha Patwardhan
9. Dr Kishore Ranade
10. Dr Mohan Agashe
11. Professor V.V. Nathan
12. Dr Suresh Gokhale
13. Dr Vidya Gokhale
14. Rachel Wade

Cover and chapter photo credits:

Photos by Sudheer Barve
Models for photographs depicting the following emotional moods:

1. Peace—Evie Charles
2. Wonder—Iris Bee You Lee-Lo
3. Disgust—Meenakshi Paranjpe
4. Humour—Mike Baldwin
5. Anger—Laurel Zachary

6. Courage—Dr Parag Tambe
7. Sorrow—Sehrish Ijaz
8. Fear—Shashank Patwardhan
9. Love/beauty/delight—Sonali Tahasildar

# Three-dimensional Emotion Management (3-DEM) Framework

# The Triangle of Emotion Management

The answer to managing emotional moods cannot lie in a single aspect of behaviour. It is a confluence of the following three: (a) management science (b) medical science and (c) the arts. And to ensure that the toolbox is firmly embedded in our minds and we understand the contribution of each of these fields of expertise, we turn to three characters who are part of our first story—the three Dr Reddys:

1. Ira, who has a doctorate in management
2. Latha, who has a doctorate in Indian classical dance
3. Dr Reddy, who is a psychiatrist

## The story of the quitter and the 3-DEM

2014, London.

Quitting a job was not something Mark wanted. And it wasn't something that happened overnight. It was an outcome of the series of thoughts jostling in Mark's overcrowded mind for a long time.

As much as Mark tried to ignore it, a voice in his mind continued to niggle him. It was in his head as he was travelling to work every day, it drummed on when he was in meetings, beat on when he was at home trying to juggle between giving time to a new born baby and handling calls from work.

Every time Mark told the voice to shut up, the voice came back with a vengeance,

'You should just quit', or in disguise, it whispered 'Work on that idea of yours', 'Go on, do something that makes you more fulfilled', 'Your family hates your working lifestyle and you should quit'.

Mark had been contemplating quitting, but when he did quit, he had embarked on an awful adventure, like riding a tiger that is out of control and would consume him if he got off. Mark did sense that listening to the voice was the biggest mistake he could make, which he did anyway.

But why did Mark quit?

What was worse was that he did not tell his wife about it. Every morning, he got dressed in his suit and left home as if he was going to work. Every day he stopped at Waterloo station, and sat at the same table in the same café looking for jobs and staring numbly at his bank account which would run dry in another 2 months.

Mark was a bright and talented professional. What he was trying to grapple with was 'Did he quit because he wanted something better and fulfilling or had he just gone insane?'

Mark knew he was running away from something. Boring work, nagging people at the workplace, the family not supporting him, or just for a reason that just could not be articulated. He did not have the time to figure out; he was desperate for a job to get some money in his account. Life at this point was not about reflection but about paying the bills.

Mark was thinking of all the reasons why he quit work, the demanding job, demanding family and work balance. Maybe he made a mistake, but what if it was the right thing to do?

At the moment he quit, Mark could sense that he could be making an error of judgement. But what he did not anticipate is the feeling that hit him and stayed with him for long—regret. Regret hit him hard and on the face.

Mark decided to find some help to get through what he considered to be an emotional black out. He wasn't sure what the answer was—a therapist, a coach or a psychologist.

He remembered his friend was going to a life coach on a regular basis, but his ego told him not to contact him for a reference. No one knew he had lost his job and he believed no one needed to know that he needed 'mental' help. It's quite amazing how, even during times of despair, the ego can stay with a human being.

It was week 4. Mark had been sitting at the cafe at Waterloo station skimming for jobs on the internet clicking page after page. It was peak time, and Mark was feeling uncomfortable watching everyone suited up, standing in a line to grab their coffee. Mark was suited up but had no workplace to go to.

A tall man with greying curls walked up to Mark's table with his massive tray loaded with two chocolate croissants, one large coffee and a chocolate muffin. The gentleman paused at Mark's table and opened the conversation with a broad smile,

'Excuse me, do you mind if I share your table?' Mark had no other option but to nod.

Mark did not want to have any conversation with anyone, but the gentleman carried on,

'Hi, my name is Reddy,' he said in heavily accented English.

Mark half-smiled. Dr Reddy took a bite of his scrumptious croissant and said, 'I have been noticing you for the last 4 days. Haven't seen one of you for a long time since 2008.'

Mark was pretty much offended now,

'Listen Mr, I don't know you and I am not up for a chat. And, what exactly do you mean by "one of me Mr Reddy!"'

Dr Reddy paused and then replied 'Dr, It's Dr Reddy. Sorry to offend you but what I meant by one of you goes back to the banking crisis days. In 2008, after the banking crisis there were so many bankers who were made redundant and so many suits in coffee shops all over the city looking for jobs. Most of them had not informed their family, with the hope they will find something soon. And you my friend tick all the boxes of how they behaved and gave it away.'

Mark was surprised by how Dr Reddy knew so much about what he was doing through. Mark wanted to know more and blurted,

'How do you know so much about me?'

Dr Reddy explained,

'I am a psychiatrist and I happened to be doing some research on emotions at the workplace around 2008. The whole of this impressive City of London became my research lab. Nothing like studying bankers who are otherwise meant to be emotionally cold, being jobless and their emotions ripped to pieces. There is a mind inside that suit and it has emotions struggling to be let out.'

'Executives just like you were sitting in this very cafe with sad faces trying to figure out what had hit them. I spoke to some of them, to listen to what they were going through. Some of them still showed the fake side where they may be saying positive things but their eyes gave it away. At the end of a session, some even shed tears!'

'What are you doing here?'

Mark replied, 'I am drinking coffee, just like you?'

Dr Reddy laughed, 'I can see that. Also, you have been coming to this cafe for the last 4 days, no one meets you but you are there with some hope on your face. What is it that your mind is looking for? Outside in this world there is a plethora of choices, of depressing news, of sorrow. But inside your brain and body it is "the perfect code", a perfect simple harmonious set of activities.' Curious, Mark quizzed Dr Reddy on what the brain does. Dr Reddy happily delved into the hormones and 'happiness chemicals'.

Before Mark could ask his next question on whether dopamine shots are available in the market, the old doctor stood up and gave him a mischievous smile.

'You don't want to be a neurologist, do you?'

'Krish!'

'Dad!'

Mark watched as two women rushed to their table. The resemblance between them was unmistakable. The older one sported thick black eyeliner and a big red painted dot on her forehead. Dr Reddy's eyes lit up and he embraced the younger woman as if they hadn't met for years. He turned to Mark smiling broadly.

'Mark, meet the loveliest women in my Universe. My precocious, Oxford-returned management graduate Dr Ira Reddy and my confidante, the Indian classical dance scholar Dr Latha Reddy!' At this introduction, Ira rolled her eyes and Latha blushed.

Mark smiled politely and stood up to excuse himself, offering Dr Reddy the personal space that was clearly due.

'It was a pleasure meeting you Dr Reddy. Hope to see you sometime soon,' Mark extended his hand, intending to part ways. Instead of turning his attention to his family, Dr Reddy took the extended hand and turned it skyward.

'Mark, may I see your other hand too please?' he said softly, probably emboldened by the familiarity of the past hour. Mark extended his other hand as well casting a furtive look at other occupants of the coffee shop. Engrossed in their laptops or phones, nobody seemed to have the time or inclination to grant him a second glance. Dr Reddy turned Mark's other palm skywards and placed Latha's hand over his palm, in touching distance but not touching.

'Weigh the science of emotion in one palm and the art in the other Mark. Think of your mind as a musical instrument and the thoughts as music. To produce good music, you need to know how to play the musical instrument, not necessarily rip apart the musical instrument to understand the mechanics of how it works. If something is grossly wrong with a musical instrument, it needs a technician to fix it and back at the hospital, that's what we do. But to just tune this musical instrument and get it to produce coherent music, the harmony between the art and science is enough! Ira—could I have your palm please?'

Ira was not amused but indulged her father, knowing his penchant for 'good causes'.

Dr Reddy placed Ira's palm close to Mark's forehead, again within touching distance but not touching him.

Mark hated any invasion of privacy. Nobody, except the perpetuators of his job loss knew about his current situation and he was not about to change that. On the London tube, at tube stations, on escalators, Mark tried his best to maintain some distance between his body and co-passengers. He was especially wary of people dressed in exotic attire. At this moment, Mark could inhale Ira's cool scent, unmistakably Armani and Latha's sandalwood perfume, clearly not expensive but mystic in its own way. Even as Mark was deeply conscious of how much he had allowed a stranger to invade his personal space in the past hour, Dr Reddy's soft voice scaled a few octaves.

'And the third dimension my friend, is this fascinating world of management science that Ira gets her DPhil in. From this management science, we get a simple five-point formula for managing emotion.'

Dr Reddy continued,

'Curiously, this social science grows and flourishes as it seems to borrow from so many other disciplines. Few years ago, our psychology Guru Daniel Kanheman even won the Nobel prize for Economics! Then these leadership types use drama, draw brain and mind maps and what not!'

Dr Reddy was smiling warmly at Ira, probably revelling in the moment a parent connects with an offspring at the intellectual level.

'So, Mark, the answers to managing emotion at the workplace then lie at the confluence of our three disciplines—medical science, ancient Indian art theories and management science. It is only when one gleans the relevant aspects of each of these and yearns to find ones' balance, the journey towards (as Ira says) the "anti-fragile" begins.'

Dr Reddy ended his soliloquy with a nod to Ira. By this time, the so far aloof Ira was more engaged. The 'anti-fragile' was her favourite term from her favourite professor at Said Business School—Dr Bent Flyvbjerg. And Bent, as he was popularly known, used it beautifully in the context of mega-project management. With true academic discipline, Bent directed his students to the books of the legendary economist who coined the term—Nassim Taleb. Before Ira could pick up her father's cue and explain the anti-fragile, Latha spoke for the first time,

'That is how the river of knowledge flows, through generations of scholars and that is why the classics are called classics—they stand the test of time and endure the vagaries of contemporary fads to still say what is the eternal truth—across, time, ages, countries, cultures— and that is exactly the case with our nine emotional moods—our *Navarasas.*'

She smiled, her tiny white teeth gleaming.

'Anti-fragile? Nine emotional moods?' the eternal know-all through his high-flying career, Mark would ordinarily be piqued at being 'out of the loop' especially when not two but three people seemed to know what they were talking about. Mark's normal response would have been to pretend to be half-listening and then quietly run a web search on his phone to ensure he was 'on the same page' with the rest. If 'being out of the loop' involved an important piece of office gossip, he would still pretend to be too busy to care and then have one of his flunkeys on the job to 'update him' on whatever it is he had missed out on. But under no circumstances would Mark ever admit that there was something he genuinely did not know.

'That sounds really interesting. We must catch up some time.' Mark pursed his lips in a half smile that reached nowhere near his eyes. 'I must get going now,' he turned to leave, having stopped himself from making the next statement that came to him naturally—'Sorry, too much on my plate now!'

'Do join us for lunch Mark. Our cerebral daughter would need some nutrition before she can lead her dad through the nuances of the anti-fragile and its nuances in work-life.' This time, it was Latha's turn to look surprised. Her husband was inviting Mark to join what was to be a cozy family meal to celebrate Ira's graduation from Said Business School. Back in India, Latha was used to Krish bringing medical college colleagues and researchers with him home and supplementing their meals with quick side-dishes so a table for two would easily be converted into a table for four. But here in London, when the two of them just left him in a café for an hour while they shopped—who was Mark? But gracious as ever, Latha quickly smiled,

'It would be lovely to have you with us Mark. Do come along, only if you don't have any other engagement of course. My husband can be quite perseverant!'

Mark hesitated. For the first time since he graduated from university, he genuinely did not have anything else to do. Going home so early was out of question and none of the recruiter calls he had been waiting for had materialized. But lunch would mean conversation, more questions on careers and what Mark did for a living. He was not ready to let two strange women know that he had no job to go to.

'Honestly I'm alright. Some other time,' said Mark, piqued at the threat to his personal space and walked away.

'Mark!' this time it was Latha.

'You seem to have other commitments. But one of my former students who relocated to the UK few years ago has organized a workshop on the nine emotional moods. I'll be conducting it in a place called Little Venice, apparently near Paddington. Would you mind if we send you an invite?'

Latha was smiling. Mark could not make out if she knew he had nothing better to do or was just being polite.

Mark was overwhelmed by the persistence and did not want to appear impolite. 'Sure, you can reach me on...' he was about to present his business card with a flourish. Mark had been immensely proud of his fancy designation and office address.

'Sorry, I've run out of business cards,' Mark pursed his lips. He picked up another paper napkin, scribbled his email address with his fancy branded ballpoint pen and handed it over to Latha.

Once again, he flashed a smile that reached nowhere near his eyes and walked away.

* * *

A few weeks later, Mark made his way to Little Venice near Paddington station, hoping he did not run into any of his former colleagues. He was not worried about running co-commuters. Even if anyone saw him or he saw them, they would all be rushing towards their next train connection. And conversation was not a thing on the London Underground, at the most a nod, with a hint of a smile may be!

As he walked into the darkened room nestled in a small garden, he saw this slide projected on the wall saying in big and bold font 'Management Science'.

Whether it is a corporate office, a doctor's clinic, a charitable organization, a construction site, an educational institution, a court of law or a performing arts/sports arena, the modern workplace demands decorum and a certain framework of work life gentility and etiquette. However strong the emotion generated by events at the workplace, the tenets of professionalism demand that the 'true professional' remains in control of his/her reaction at the (often public) moment of time. At the same time, modern-day leadership demands that leaders display strong emotional quotient, sensitivity towards their stakeholders and do not appear frigid or impassive. Therefore, the outcome expected from the usage of this toolbox is a balanced individual who does not fall prey to provocation and is, in fact, able to leverage emotion to get the best out of oneself as well as co-workers. Let us call this expected outcome 'the anti-fragile professional'. To understand what this anti-fragile is, let us turn to Ira and her takeaways from her management education (Figure 1.1).

**Figure 1.1**   The Outcome Expected When We Successfully Manage Emotions

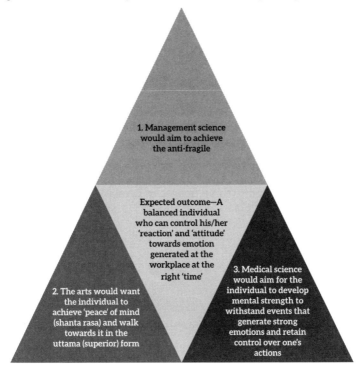

1. Management science would aim to achieve the anti-fragile

Expected outcome—A balanced individual who can control his/her 'reaction' and 'attitude' towards emotion generated at the workplace at the right 'time'

2. The arts would want the individual to achieve 'peace' of mind (shanta rasa) and walk towards it in the uttama (superior) form

3. Medical science would aim for the individual to develop mental strength to withstand events that generate strong emotions and retain control over one's actions

*Source:* Authors.

'What is the anti-fragile?'

Ira scanned the room full of eager faces for answers. There was silence.

'What is fragile?' she asked.

'Something delicate, which is likely to break...' spoke a small voice from the back.

'That's perfect, then what is the opposite of fragile?' Ira quizzed her audience further.

'Strong,' chirped someone at the front.

'What can be stronger than strong?' asked Ira with a hint of a smile.

'Unbreakable?' said the small voice again.

'What makes something unbreakable?' asked Ira flipping to this slide:

'Fragile projects, relationships and people break unless they are handled with care.'

'Robust organizations, friendships and minds withstand the vagaries of nature, external attacks and abuse. They may bruise and sometimes never heal, but they survive.'

'The true test of strength comes with anti-fragility, the willingness to welcome unexpected, high-impact events and evolve to suit the demands of time.'

Ira put up the following three images to demonstrate that strength lies in flexibility:

**Strong**

Anti-fragile

Anti-fragile

Anti-fragile then is something that becomes stronger when it endures extreme conditions like heat and can be remoulded into a new form. So, an anti-fragile person, then, first needs to rid himself/ herself of isolation and rigidity of thought. When a person opens his mind to the fact that no workplace will ever be perfect, the emotion toolbox described further becomes easy to practise:

| 1 | Acknowledge | I am not perfect and nor are my co-workers. There will be occasions when strong emotions will be generated at the workplace |
|---|---|---|
| 2 | Analyse | It will help to put into categories what I'm really feeling (see the nine emotions discussed later) and understand at least some part of what happens in the brain |
| 3 | Accept | Whatever emotion is generated, in most cases, I will not have control over the perpetuator of those emotions |
| 4 | Administer | I will 'choose' my attitude |
| 5 | Act | I will 'follow' my plan |

Ira handed over the following emotion management toolbox to each of the participants:

> 1. Acknowledge—You are feeling something
> 2. Analyse—What are you feeling?
> 3. Accept—It is difficult to not feel this way
> 4. Administer—Your strategy to respond in the appropriate way
> 5. Act—Out your response to achieve the outcome you want

'And before I hand over to our medical doctor, let's do a simple exercise to help us walk closer towards our own "anti-fragile selves". Can anyone tell me what is a Black Swan?'

A hand went up and an enthusiastic voice squeaked,

'I've watched the movie about the ballet dancer!'

Ira smiled the smile of a trainer who receives expected answers class after class.

'Oh yes, there's a movie, but has anyone heard of a book by that name?'

'Taleb? Some management book?' a hesitant voice in the audience uttered.

'Yes! *The Black Swan* by Nassim Taleb (2008) speaks about high-impact, unexpected events, that's right!' said Ira.

She continued,

'In ancient Europe, nobody had even seen a black swan. So, they thought only white swans existed. There was an old European saying which likened the black swan to the impossible. Until one day, someone spotted a black swan in New Zealand. Suddenly, the old saying made no sense because the "impossible" became a "rare" but possibly foreseeable event. Taleb has brilliantly applied this concept to high-impact, unexpected events that could derail business projects.

My professor Dr Bent Flyvbjerg applied it to "embracing black swans" when they happen so as to learn from them, in order to prevent them in the future,' said Ira. She then elaborated on how unknown risk can be acknowledged, analyzed and converted to anticipated risk. And we are applying the concept to our emotion management toolbox.

When someone at the workplace lets you down for the first time in your life, you feel immensely sad, but you are also shocked, so you feel worse. If someone steals credit from your team for the first time, you feel angry and it is worse because you just did not know people could do that and get away with it in work life! When you deal with the perpetuator of this emotion the second time over, you anticipate that they may steal credit and would either take precautions or "choose" to ignore them. But this time, the black swan is not a black swan, it is a grey swan and you already have a contingency plan in place to deal with the risk. So, in the context of emotion too, every time you face something negative and deal with it, it is making you stronger and you are walking closer to becoming that "anti-fragile, balanced individual" that you want to be!

Now, to be able to use this toolbox defined by our conceptual management science and analyse why we experience what we do, let us turn to medical science. Over to my father, the medical doctor!' Ira concluded.

# Medical Science

The eldest Dr Reddy smiled broadly, his keen eyes boring into the soul-searchers in the audience.

'Outside in this world there is a plethora of choices, of depressing news, of sorrow. But inside your brain and body there is "the perfect code", a perfect simple harmonious set of activities.' Dr Reddy pulled out his business card that had the image of a brain on one side. He placed it on the overhead projector he insisted on still using. The image looked like that shown in Figure 1.2.

He continued, pointing towards the image on the card.

'The brain is complex in structure so humans can make their life simple. No smartphone in the world can beat that.

**Figure 1.2**   The Simple Brain Diagram

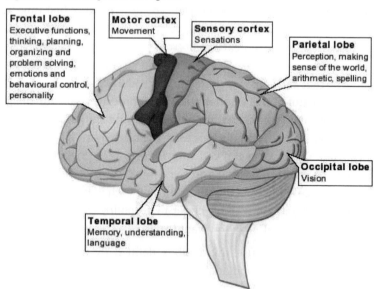

In the field of emotion research, there have been a vast number of definitions that have been proposed over the last 100 years since Charles Darwin's seminal book (Darwin 2012), written in 1872, *The Expression of Emotions in Man and Animals*. This book established that emotions serve an important evolutionary purpose: Fear evokes the need for protection leading to the response of fight or flight and the emotions of love/lust result in reproduction. This brings us to the concept of the lizard brain.'

## The Lizard Brain Versus the Limbic System

The brain stem, cerebellum and basal ganglia are casually referred to as your 'lizard brain'. These parts handle basic body functions such as breathing, balance and coordination and simple survival urges such as feeding, mating and defence.

But mammals have more complex emotions. Our emotions are processed in several regions that together are loosely called the 'limbic system' (Figure 1.3). They form a ring around our 'lizard brain' regions, which evolved earlier. Mammal brains also have an outer layer called a cortex, which helps us control our emotions and make complex decisions.

The size of the cerebral cortex (in proportion with the rest of the brain) is larger in humans than other mammals. This cerebral cortex handles many of our highly complex skills such as language and problem-solving.

Mammals tend to have strong emotional bonds with family members, and they generally care for their young ones after birth. Instead of responding just by reflex and instinct (as a lizard does when it snaps at you if you get too close) they are guided by their emotions, making their behaviour more flexible. Mammals tend to have good memories, especially for events that created strong emotions.

**Figure 1.3**  The Limbic System

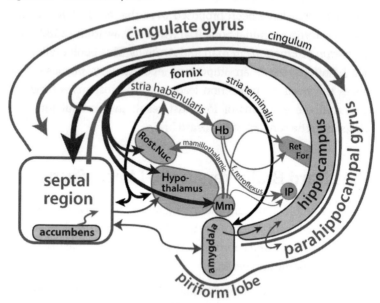

*Source:* http://vanat.cvm.umn.edu/fletcher/pages/limbicComponents.html (accessed on 26 June 2018).

Part of the brain's information-processing network includes neurons or cells that transmit signals throughout the brain. Neurons send signals through neurotransmitters, which are chemicals some release and others receive. These chemicals essentially let the parts of the brain communicate with each other.

The three most commonly studied neurotransmitters are dopamine, serotonin and norepinephrine.

When we learn, the brain undergoes changes and it's just not in the form of additional sulci and gyri. This phenomenon is known as 'brain plasticity'. By studying changes in the brains of animals like rats as they learn tasks, researchers have discovered that 'synapses' (the connections between neurons) and the blood cells that support neurons grow and increase in number.

If neurons are damaged or lost, they can't grow back—but the 'synapses', or connections between neurons, can. Essentially, the brain creates new pathways between neurons. In addition, areas of the brain not originally associated with some functions can take over and allow the person to relearn how to do things.

At any given moment, dozens of chemical messengers, or neurotransmitters, are active. Some of these neurotransmitters go between individual cells, while others are broadcast to entire brain regions. By layering signals on other signals, your brain can adjust how you respond to things and can effectively alter your mood. If you're in danger, for example, your brain releases stress hormones that make you react faster, flooding certain regions with the neurotransmitter epinephrine (adrenaline). When the danger subsides, your brain sends out a calming signal in the form of chemicals that dampen the response of regions that create fear.

Just as hunger motivates you to find food, emotions motivate you to take care of other needs—such as safety and companionship—that ultimately promote survival and reproduction.

## Complexity of Human Emotion

Psychologists define emotions as a combination of cognitions, feelings and actions. This means what we think of as 'emotions' includes not only how we feel but also how we process and respond to those feelings.

The human brain is made of a 100 billion nerve cells. There are over 600 words in English to describe the basic emotions and we use 42 muscles in our faces to express them!

Humans are also especially sensitive to social emotions such as shame, guilt and pride, which require understanding of what other people think and feel about us—a specialty of our advanced prefrontal cortex.

Although it is true that there is no single definition, there is consensus regarding the key elements of what emotion is, as well as what emotions are not. Emotions are triggered by an individual's interpretation of an event.

When emotions are triggered, they elicit reactions in many bodily systems. They can increase our heart rate or make us sweat. Emotions are often shown on the face, the voice or the body. Although these expressions are genetically based, in adults, they are strongly influenced by culture. Thus, our natural tendency to eject an awful tasting food item will be restrained when we are served—to name an example—Brussel's sprouts or bitter gourd for dinner at our boss' home. We may even manage to smile. Importantly, emotions communicate information. Thus, sadness communicates a sense of loss, whereas anger communicates the presence of an obstacle. Emotions are adaptive; they are processes that allow us to respond to changing environmental and social challenges. And finally, emotions are not irrational. In fact, to behave rationally we need emotions.

So, the question is how do you feel when something happens at work. 'Why did this happen?' 'Have you acknowledged that it has triggered strong emotion in you?' And 'Why do you feel the way you feel about it?' Let's add another layer: 'How do you want to feel?' Worded differently, this still goes back to the five As of the toolbox Ira described.

Everything we do is usually trying to get to one outcome, 'happiness'. Our happiness—down to a few chemicals (Figure 1.4).

**Figure 1.4**   The Happiness Chemicals Cartoon

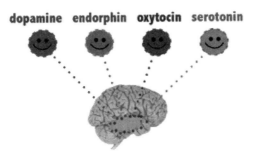

*Source:* https://www.slideshare.net/LorettaBreuning/rewire-your-natural-happy-brain-chemicals-dopamine-serotonin-oxytocin-endorphin (accessed on 26 June 2018).

As Simon Sinek[1] puts it, here are the happiness chemicals:

1.  Endorphin: It diminishes our perceptions of what we call pain and keeps us going that extra mile when we workout. Good for those late nights.

2.  Dopamine: What motivates us? Specific targets that inspire us to get rewarded. It is the greedy function of our brain. Makes us feel good, makes us feel high. Highly addictive, like smoking, alcohol or any other addiction.

3.  Serotonin: The need to feel significance, pride, status. This is what we need, recognition. 'I am doing it for my family, business, the world and so on.' It reinforces the sense of relationships, human-to-human contact.

4.  Oxytocin: It generates intimacy, trust, feeling that someone will protect us—mother, father, the army, alpha male or female. We feel this when we are protected and loved—the feeling of safety.

---

[1]  https://accelerole.com/simon-sinek-leaders-eat-last-model-cooperation-inspired-biology-atd-key-learning/ (accessed on 16 June 2018).

Antidepressant drugs alter how the brain processes serotonin, a neurotransmitter linked to feelings of serenity and optimism. These drugs, called selective serotonin reuptake inhibitors (SSRIs), increase levels of serotonin in the synapse by blocking its removal.

As Dr Reddy concluded his fascinating presentation, he scanned the room. Some people had zoned out, unconcerned with what went on in the brain if it worked for them! Others had been taking copious notes and appeared exhausted by the effort. Sensing the desperate need for a break, Dr Reddy gestured to Ira to 'relieve his audience' with some tea!

## The Performing Arts

Back in the room after the much-needed break, the audience was curious to see Latha in her resplendent deep purple sari, her kohl lined eyes appearing bigger than ever before due to the thick eyeliner and the deep maroon perfect dot on her forehead. With an invocatory purposeful look, upwards and touching the ground beneath her to seek forgiveness from Mother Earth for stamping on the surface as she explained, Latha began her demonstration of the *Navarasas*—the nine emotional moods.

*The Natyashastra*, written by the scholar Bharata Muni, is an ancient Indian text dated between 2nd century BC and 2nd century AD which analyses all aspects of performing art. *The Natyashastra* describes *Navarasas* or nine *rasas* (moods) that are the basis of all human emotions. Each *rasa* encompasses not just the emotion, but also the various things that cause that emotion. These two things go hand in hand and are impossible to treat separately. This duality is part of every *rasa* to varying degrees.

According to Bharata, there are eight *rasas* (four positive and four negative) and this was accepted till Uddhata, the first commentator

**Figure 1.5**   The Nine Types of Emotional Flavours/Moods

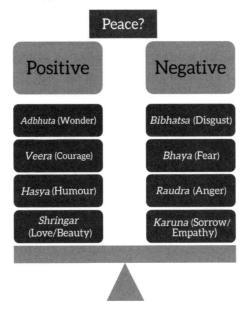

Source: Authors.

on the *Natyashastra*, began to speak of *rasa* as nine in number (Figure 1.5). The aim of the arts (all forms such as drama, music, dance, sculpture, painting) has been to evoke the *rasa* in the one who experiences the art.

The Sanskrit word *rasa* literally means flavour, juice or essence. In languages like Marathi, it is also used to denote 'interest' or taste.

Thus, it could be best translated as the aesthetic feeling that is created in the spectator when he/she witnesses an effective presentation of the art. *Rasa* is about human state of mind. It is about what the mind feels and the expression of the feeling thereafter. In Bharata's *Natyashastra*, *rasa* is an emotion experienced by the audience created by the facial expression or the *bhava* of the actor. In Indian classical dance, it is referred to as *rasa-abhinaya*. If *bhava* is produced, *rasa* will manifest.

A certain mood comes and stays, even though its cause is gone, for example, in the modern work context, a mobile ringing in a critical client meeting or the impact of one bad presentation on the rest.

Bharata's *Natyashastra* gives the following Rasa Sutra:

'Vibhaavanubhaavyabhichaarisanyogaadrasanishpattihi ll'

That is, the combination of *vibhava* (determinant factors), *anubhava* (consequents) and *vyabhicharibhava* (complementary psychological states) leads to *rasa*.

1. *Shringar* means love and beauty resulting in delight or pleasure. This is the emotion used to represent that which appeals to the human mind, that which one finds beautiful, that which evokes love. This is indeed the king of all *rasas* and the one that finds the most frequent portrayal in art. It can be used for the love between friends, the love between a parent and a child, the love for god or the love between a guru (mentor) and his disciples.

2. *Hasya* is the *rasa* used to express joy or mirth. It can be used to depict simple light-heartedness or riotous laughter and everything in between. Teasing and laughing with a friend, being amused and carefree or simply feeling frivolous and naughty—these are all facets of *hasya*. At the modern workplace, humour could also find form in mirth, laughter or sarcasm.

3. *Bibhatsa* is disgust, the emotion evoked by anything that nauseates, revolts or sickens us. When something comes to our notice that is coarse and graceless, beneath human dignity or even consideration, we feel like giving up or moving away from it.

4. *Raudra* is anger and all its forms. *Raudra* is probably the most violent of *rasas*.

5. *Veera* is heroism, courage, bravery and self-confidence.

6. *Bhaya* is fear. It could manifest in anxiety, helplessness, panic, timidity or dread.

7. *Karuna* is grief, sorrow, sympathy and compassion.

8. *Adbhuta* is wonder and curiosity or the appreciation of a marvel.

9. *Shanta* is serenity, peace and the state of calm and unruffled repose that is marked simply by the lack of all other *rasas*. Because all emotions are absent in *shanta* there is controversy whether it is a *rasa* at all. *Shanta* is what Buddha felt when he was enlightened, when he reached the higher spiritual plane that led him to salvation or nirvana and freed him from the cycle of life and death. *Shanta* represents complete harmony between the mind, body and the universe.

The ancient Indian texts also classify characters in a performance or story as per their thought process, demeanour, upbringing, culture and thus behaviour and reactions to different situations. There are three degrees:

1. *Uttama* (high): Usually accorded to the Gods and Goddesses in mythology or highly evolved human beings who would be above the ordinary display of unbridled emotion. They would maintain their dignity irrespective of provocation.

2. *Madhyama* (medium): Ordinary human beings who would display emotions as they find appropriate for the situation. They would not make any effort to rise above the ordinary.

3. *Adhama* (low): Usually accorded to demons and human beings with low education/culture. These people would be given to loud behaviour and would show little or no restraint in expressing their emotions in public.

As Latha finished her engaging demonstration amidst applause, her husband and daughter joined her on the dais to bring together the confluence of the three fields and establish their context in the application of the emotion management toolbox. Ira flipped open a new slide showing the following table and Dr Reddy spoke:

'This is what the three spokes of our triangle of emotion management bring together—we have each of the nine emotional moods or *rasas*, we have their dependent/related emotions, we have the medical explanation in brief for the related ones.'

| No. | Sanskrit Name | English Name | Nuances | Science—What Happens |
|-----|---------------|--------------|---------|----------------------|
| 1. | *Shringar* | Love and beauty | Team spirit, nurturing, respect, amicable relationships at the workplace | Dopamine is related to experiences of pleasure and the reward-learning process. In other words, when you do something good, you're rewarded with dopamine and gain a pleasurable, happy feeling. This teaches your brain to want to do it again and again. |
| 2. | *Hasya* | Humour | Sarcasm, laughter, satire | |
| | | | | Oxytocin would promote 'work chemistry'. |
| 3. | *Adbhuta* | Wonder | Admiration, outlandish goals and vision | Serotonin is a neurotransmitter associated with memory and learning. Researchers believe it plays a part in the regeneration of brain cells, which has been linked to easing depression and triggering action. |
| 4. | *Veera* | Courage | Heroism, accomplishment, satisfaction on achievement, self-actualization | |

| No. | Sanskrit Name | English Name | Nuances | Science—What Happens |
|---|---|---|---|---|
| 5. | *Karuna* | Pathos | Sorrow, sympathy, empathy, compassion, pain, insult, hurt, low self-esteem, shame | An imbalance in serotonin levels results in an increase in anger, anxiety, depression and panic. |
| 6. | *Bhaya* | Fear | Anxiety, apprehension, panic | |
| 7. | *Krodha* | Terror | Anger, insult, attack on self-esteem, loss of faith | |
| 8. | *Bibhatsa* | Disgust | Odious, urge to flee from the situation | |
| 9. | *Shanta* | Peace | Calm, balance, acceptance, all black swans converted to white swans | Norepinephrine helps moderate your mood by controlling stress and anxiety. |

# What Is the Outcome You Want to Achieve?

Based on these principles, in order to demonstrate optimum professional behaviour even in the face of extreme provocation, one would like to achieve the following:

- Anti-fragile
- Ability to anticipate black swans
- Control over one's words, actions, judgement, decision-making,
- *Uttama*, *madhyama*, *adhama*—what does the situation deserve? What does the *vibhav* (the cause and its perpetuator) deserve? What will you gain from the response?

## The Tools

The Five As:

1. Acknowledge what you are really feeling.
2. Analyse why—*vibhav*—you are feeling this way. What are the factors that have contributed to this feeling?
3. Accept—You don't agree, but accept that it happened and then create distance, so acknowledge, accept but do not identify or become one with the emotion.
4. Administer—Evaluate what you can control/change and accept what you cannot. Decide your line of action.
5. Act—Counter with opposing *rasas*, remind your ego of the promise.

## The Solution

*Rasa* sadhana (emotional fasting) creates distance between emotion and yourself by promising to stay away—promise yourself, establish rules, practise for short periods and then go on for longer periods. First practise actions, emails, words, then graduate to thoughts. For example, following is the exhaustive analysis of one of the emotional moods—*raudra* or anger:

| Vibhav (Cause) | Sthahi Bhav (Dominant Emotion) | Anubhava (Experience) | Vyabhichari (Related Emotions) | Response | | |
|---|---|---|---|---|---|---|
| | | | | Uttama (High) | Madhyama (Medium) | Adhama (Low) |
| Betrayal, unfulfilled expectation | Anger (krodha) | Anger such as burning eyes and heaving chest | Jealousy, insult, hurt, desire to harm the person | Walking away from the situation | Sarcasm, subtly disguised expression of anger | Swearing, physical attack, shouting, back-biting, spreading rumours |

The solution for each will be proposed along with the analysis under each of the nine chapters for the nine emotions.

# References

Darwin, C. 2012. *The Expression of the Emotions in Man and Animals.*

Taleb, Nassim Nicholas. 2008, February 28. *The Black Swan: The Impact of the Highly Improbable—With a New Section: On Robustness and Fragility (Incerto).* Paperback. New York: Random House.

CHAPTER
**2**

# Survey Results and Analysis

We did a survey to understand the role that people think emotions play at the workplace. We had about 600 responses of which 44 per cent were male and 56 per cent were female. Majority of participants were between 35 and 44 years old. Those who held at least a master's degree were 50 per cent followed by 35 per cent with a bachelor's degree.

Mid-level managers were 35 per cent and seniors were 18 per cent. Self-employed were 20 per cent.

Majority of the responses were from United Kingdom, India and United States. And few responses were from UAE, Australia, Canada and Singapore.

Out of these, as shown in the following figure, 95 per cent have felt strong emotions at workplace. That is a very high percentage busting the myth around the belief at workplace 'Nothing personal, it is just business!'

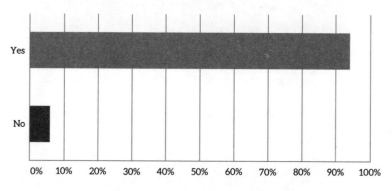

The percentage of those who had issues while managing emotions at workplace was 54 per cent:

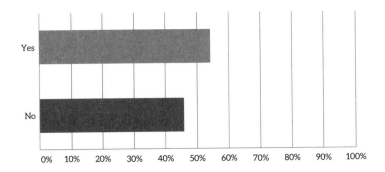

The percentage of those who have been negatively impacted by emotions they felt at workplace was 58 per cent:

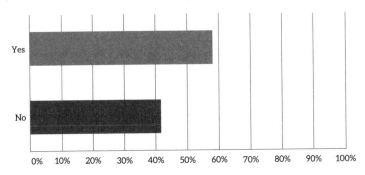

The percentage of those who had quit their jobs because they were struggling with negative emotions at the workplace was 34 per cent:

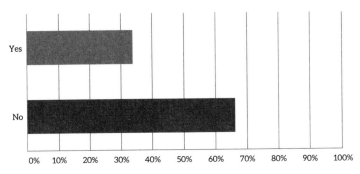

As shown in the following figure, a high percentage of those who left their job felt that anger followed by a feeling of disgust was the main reason for them leaving the workplace. This is a very important finding as the mood of 'disgust' is a culmination of a prolonged period of a negative emotion such as fear, anger or sorrow.

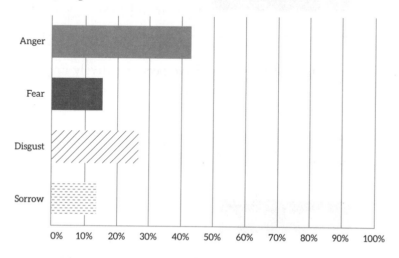

The percentage of those who felt that they did not have adequate support at the workplace to deal with strong emotions generated at the workplace was 46 per cent:

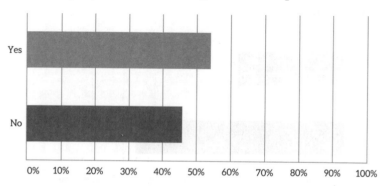

The percentage of those who felt that they would benefit from improved support and resources to deal with strong emotions at the workplace was 80 per cent:

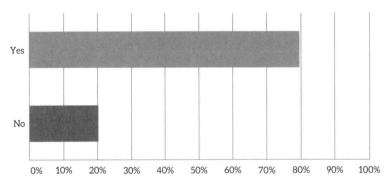

On being asked what kind of support would they like, a very high percentage were keen on getting in-house support in the form of an empathetic manager or work buddy:

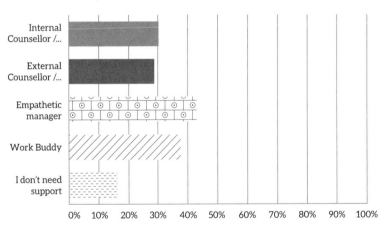

The percentage of those who agreed that they use emotions proactively to improve productivity at work was 64 per cent, as shown in the following figure. This would be to leverage the impact of the four positive emotional moods—love/beauty, humour, wonder and courage.

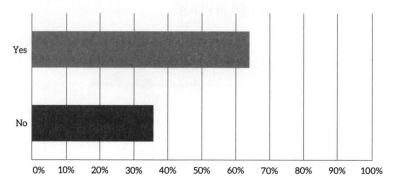

# Love

*To be successful, the first thing to do is fall in love with your work.*

—Sister Mary Lauretta

# The Manifestation of Love and Beauty

The survey revealed the following results. Out of the individuals surveyed,

- 64 per cent used or leveraged emotions at work to improve productivity.
- 68 per cent used delight/love/beauty successfully or leveraged these emotions to improve the pace or quality of work.

## Depicting 'Love/Beauty' in the Arts

In the narrow sense, *shringar* is translated as erotic love, romantic love, attraction or beauty. In the broader sense, it could be creating a positive atmosphere, a 'rehearsal for the culmination' and defeating the enemy *rasas* (fear, anger, disgust, sadness).

The predominant emotional mood of love/beauty (*shringar* as defined in the Indian arts) has several transitionary/ temporary emotions associated with it. In Indian classical dance or theatre, the expression of 'love' is usually depicted with a soft expression, the eyes mellow, the lips upturned in a soft smile, the hands, arms, shoulders appear poised to reach out to the object of beauty or love. The body language depicting 'being attracted towards the situation' is of prime importance as the core of love/beauty is 'getting lost in the emotion and the desire for more of the same'.

## 'Love/Beauty' in Science

Biologically, love/beauty is one of the manifestations of a highly positive mood when faced with a series of desirable/

attractive objects/situations/behaviours. When the body is faced with something desirable such as tasty food, a joyous occasion, physical beauty, respect and praise, the natural body reaction is to want more of the same. Repeated instances and associations lead to the manifestation of the positive endocrines (happiness chemicals) and the instances of 'losing track of time' in this happy state. It also leads to a state of oblivion where the 'engrossed person or people' have no idea what others around them are doing or observing.

The emotion of 'love' or 'liking' of the workplace and its people facilitate the secretion of dopamine and the other 'happiness endocrines', leading to a feeling of general well-being and joy, often colloquially described as 'being on a high'. When one feels this 'high' is a result of people and relationships at the workplace, it is bound to contribute to a positive feeling towards work and, in most cases, high productivity.

## Depicting 'Love' at the Workplace

The mood of 'love' though present at the workplace is rarely acknowledged as love. Given the increasingly one-track depictions of love in the world of social media (where love is singularly romantic and sexual in nature), the 'keeping away of love' from the workplace appears to be the most appropriate thing to do. To support this even more are the most avoidable cases of sexual harassment at the workplace and the lack of awareness, ability and sometimes willingness to differentiate between 'good touch' and 'bad touch'.

But people who have evolved to have the confidence to acknowledge 'love' without necessarily attaching a romantic/sexual connotation to it are able to leverage all the positives associated with this emotion for a highly productive and happy workplace.

The power of love (even at the workplace) is so strong that it is often a culmination of positive events/actions/triggers built up over several weeks/months and in some cases years. 'Love' would then be a result of the three prolonged emotional moods:

1. *Humour:* Sustained humour at the workplace leads to the formation of amicable relationships. In a gradual manner (and if it is not forced or done simply because it is part of HR policy!), humour can lead to colleagues finding their energizers/refreshers within the workplace without needing external relaxants during work hours. The simplicity of this emotion is that if you like your colleagues, they do not threaten or intimidate you, it is so much easier to get work done!

2. *Love is not just love towards your colleagues but the love for the work itself:* Look at the most successful performers/sportspersons of the world. While a lot of us in our professions may work silently and in isolation, the work of the 'Stars' is visible for the world to witness. And the deep love each of these outstanding people have for their work itself (not just for the adulation it brings along with it) is what is evident in their body language and facial expressions and is the core reason why they excel at what they do. This 'love' for what they do and the people they influence culminates into the single quality that separates the 'excellent' from the 'outstanding'—Passion!

In sports arenas, dance and music performances and on screen, we capture moments of people enjoying their time at work. These are exceptional individuals who have given their 'job' their best shot. So, deep is their love for their work, their vocation is synonymous with them as people.

## Love and beauty at the workplace— Rati's story

15 May 2008, Mumbai.

On a warm, rainy morning, Rati stood outside the ancient building in South Mumbai that was to be her workplace. This was one of the most expensive addresses in the city and possibly in India and most of the world. The real estate prices here are on par with London, New York and Tokyo. The building had bits of paint peeling off that had been appropriately patched up and painted by the building manager. The exterior had acquired a darkened hue characteristic of old (and often newer) buildings in the coastal city. The humidity, annual heavy rain, dirt and pollution refused to let anything look new for too long. And like everything else in Mumbai, how you looked did not matter all that much—what mattered is what you did, how and when!

Despite the recent personal upheavals in her life, Rati looked up at the building with hope and a strange sense of empathy. If this structure could withstand the vagaries of the weather, the onslaught of the salty sea air close by and still support the livelihoods of the thousands who milled in and out, could her battered old self, hold up too? Even more strange was the fact that next to her stood the two people she loved the most in her life including the one who had hurt her the most. As she stood on the curb of that busy street, her five-year-old son Malay entwined his tiny, chubby fingers in hers. Her soon-to-be ex-husband Ashay gently extricated Malay's fingers from hers and said,

'Malay, it is Mamma's first day at work. Just like it will be your first day at your new school soon. Wish her luck and we need to leave now. She needs to go!'

As the tears welled up in Rati's eyes, all over again, she ruffled Malay's tight dark curls, bent down to tie his shoelaces one last time and strode towards the entrance.

Her trepidation seemed to melt away when she was greeted by the receptionist with a warm smile,

'Rati, right? Meeta and John are expecting you. Could you just sign here please? Here's your temporary access card. HR will get your ID card made over the next few days.'

Pleasantly surprised by the speed of everything that was happening (especially after her last job as a multinational corporation when she found herself waiting for 90 minutes at the reception on Day 1 after a terrible struggle with the recruitment manager who had insisted she join the very day as there was too much work pending), Rati was even more surprised to see a short, stocky woman in a simple, pale peach outfit walk up,

'Hi Rati, I'm Meeta. Great to see you in person after that phone interview. Let's go straight to see John in his room. As you know, he is traveling this afternoon,' Rati could only smile back as she followed Meeta across the corridor. This was her new boss and she had come out to welcome her at reception! John the CEO had asked her to come in a day earlier to see him as he would be out of the country for the next 15 days. The wimp Rati reported to in her earlier organization used to ask her to send him a meeting request even if she wanted to quickly check something with him (when he sat right across the next bay doing precious little on most days!). Well, the pace at which things were moving today, the wimp could be a faint memory soon!

The meeting with John and Meeta was a blur as were the next two days. Rati and Meeta would be zipping in and out of meetings, conference calls, furiously taking notes, capturing information, churning it in their minds, both ready to attack the action points they meticulously noted down in their notebooks. At the end of day 2, Rati walked up to their desks with her sugarless cappuccino and Meeta's masala tea with two sugar cubes. Meeta smiled at her broadly,

'You know Rati, I feel as if we've been working together for 2 months instead of 2 days! I'm traveling next week too. Can you work with HR to complete the recruitment of our team? You've understood what we are trying to achieve with this special business transformation unit. When I'm back in 2 weeks, I'll meet the candidates you shortlist and we'll roll out the offers.'

Over the next two weeks, Rati met 39 candidates, some sourced by the recruitment team, others through her own personal and professional networks. She designed a brief writing test that the communication executives and managers went through before the interview. The engineers were asked to summarize a technical case study in layperson's terms. Those who fared well in these tests had brief, 40-minute interviews mainly focusing on the purpose of the business transformation unit and whether they had the enthusiasm and attitude to spur and contribute to change. Rati shortlisted seven candidates. When Meeta returned, she met each of them. Six of them were rolled out offers within two days. She requested one of them have an interview with the CEO, John. She too was rolled out an offer in a senior role.

Two months later, Meeta walked back to their adjoining desks with her masala tea and Rati's cappuccino. Both rarely got a chance to sit together peacefully. The department was buzzing with activities with a rapid turnaround on deliverables. Meeta rarely asked Rati what the team reporting to her were doing. Whenever Rati had a radical idea, she walked up to Meeta. If Meeta was travelling, she dropped her a message. Wherever Meeta was in the world, she would respond to Rati within one business day or less. If Meeta felt that the idea was too radical or she did not have the expertise or experience to take a call independently, she asked Rati to approach John (her two-up manager). Rati soon realized the sweet danger of expressing a new idea to the CEO. John would listen intently, ask a question or two and then reprimand Rati for not implementing her brilliant suggestion yet!

Among these suggestions was the first set of ideas for initiating corporate social responsibility (CSR) projects. It was the first time Rati had been formally involved in CSR. While she and her new team member Amisha explored what it was they could do first, they reached out to the people they saw every day but knew very little about the housekeeping and building security staff. Brimming over with the background research Amisha had done over the past three months, they approached their 'focus group', the house-keeping staff that toiled to keep the washrooms clean, served numerous cups of teas and coffees for the meetings that kept the organization's machinery going and tended to the manicured lawns on the company's sprawling campus.

Bright-eyed and bushy tailed Amisha sprung her first question:

'Problems with clean drinking water, sanitation, leaking hutments—there is so much that research data shows, how do you think we can help your community?'

While the others looked at each other, too overwhelmed at being asked, a petite lady in her dark blue uniform stood up and said,

'Madam, I would just like my daughter to get a job like you.' There were nods in the room, shy smiles, murmurs of approval.

Rati was stumped. The questionnaire she and Amisha had put together seemed like a pointless exercise after this. They gathered their papers and walked back to their desks. It was time for change of strategy.

Meeta was travelling so Rati emailed John with a copy to Meeta, seeking a meeting with him. The CEO listened intently and went back to his emails with a snappy response,

'Go get it done!'

In just 10 days, Amisha organized the inauguration of a basic IT (digital literacy) class for the gardeners, housekeeping and security staff, soon extending it to their families. When Meeta returned, she motivated an entire department to 'adopt' one of the IT batches to volunteer an hour of their time after work. Meeta led by example by conducting an IT class herself. The unconditional support from John and Meeta, extended to other departments too—the finance department donated old computers for the batch, the learning and development team put together a batch schedule volunteering to train 100 people in Phase 1. The classes received a resounding response and served as a trigger to transform the lives of many. A security guard who had never touched a computer before, heads security at the location and the daughter of the lady in the blue sari who stood up and spoke...well, she topped the batch and won a scholarship for an advanced level computer class! As for Rati's own mental frame of mind, she threw herself into work, enjoyed the journey and discovered her calling—CSR!

## Analysing Love at the Workplace

Like is the case with so many large organizations, Rati had worked in large global corporations where she had been just a cog in the machinery that would run happily without her. Though her contribution had been acknowledged by her immediate superiors, she was lost in the crowd and often yearned for the respect that was her due. Rati found it pleasantly refreshing to be treated with respect right from Day 1. Moreover, Meeta and John seemed to value her opinion, ideas and judgement. Most important, Meeta made it amply evident that she trusted Rati. And in an otherwise hierarchical setup that Rati had seen across organizations, Meeta seemed to have absolutely no problem with Rati approaching Meeta's own boss in her absence. The primary reason for this was Meeta's own security and confidence in her own capability and the deep trust that she and John shared.

As a result, given her own unhappy personal circumstances, the need for money to sustain herself on her own, without realizing it, Rati was seeking 'self-esteem' as well as 'love and belonging' from Maslow's pyramid and got it.

Rati's case is unusual in many ways. The progression of 'love' at the workplace is rapid and thus ridden with danger if things had not worked out well. The most critical component of this workplace scenario is that for Rati her workplace ceased to be just another source of income and she began to invest not just a great deal of time and physical effort but mental energy too. Rati began to demonstrate extreme passion for her work, the factor that differentiates excellence from outstanding.

## The Solution Matrix—3-DEM Applied to Love

As we established, the answer to managing emotion lies in the confluence of the three:

(a) the arts (b) management science (c) medical science.

# Elements of Love at the Workplace

Let us first identify the elements of love at the workplace. The following table shows the three categories of people one works with—peers, juniors and superiors.

| Co-worker | Stage 1 | Stage 2 | Stage 3 | Stage 4 If the emotional boundaries are not transcended | Stage 5 If the boundaries are transcended |
|---|---|---|---|---|---|
| **Peer** | Acknowledging a pleasant, non-threatening aura | Extending help/support for work, smooth transactions | Trust | Trusted co-worker | Friend |
| **Team member/ Junior** | Acknowledgement of competence | Appreciation of a good job done | Trust | Trusted, competent team member | Mentee |
| **Manager/ Superior** | Support for the desire to deliver professional outcome | Seeking learning, admiration | Trust | Trusted boss | Mentor |

As we can see, trust (Stage 3) is the turning point in any relationship. Once trust is established, the relationship has the opportunity to settle into a purely professional work relationship resulting in high productivity. Or if both parties allow the emotional boundary to be crossed, the relationship progresses to evolve into a bond characterized by warmth and affection for the person himself/herself—much beyond the professional. Both Stage 4 and Stage 5 are conducive to good organization culture. These are simply choices people make, how much of their emotional energy they would like to invest in the workplace, how they want to be led and how they lead.

Figure 3.1 further explores Stage 3 which is the overriding factor that contributes to building an ideal workplace—trust.

**Figure 3.1** The Ideal Ecosystem: Factors Leading to Love at and of the Workplace

**Trust**

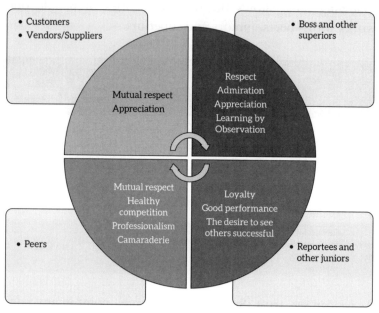

*Source:* Authors.

Figure 3.1 maps the typical ecosystem in a workplace across professions. This is the ideal set of equations among co-workers that would result in a happy workplace. However, it is highly unlikely (if not impossible) to expect these equations to exist among all stakeholders in a workplace. Emotions that attack these positive emotions are the factors mapped in Figure 3.2. The overriding factor that contributes to preventing the building of the ideal workplace is insecurity and the lack of confidence in one's own capability to succeed without walking over other people.

Figure 3.2   Workplace Factors Counter-attacking Love for the Workplace

**Insecurity**

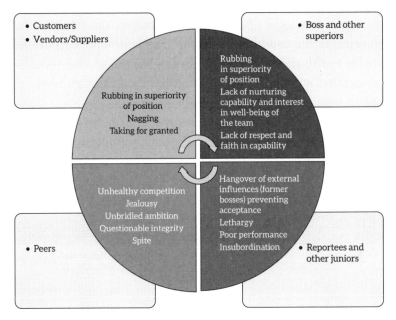

# Building the 3-DEM Action Plan: Leveraging Love at the Workplace

Leaders have built nations leveraging on the love people had for their cause and ultimately also for their leaders. The 3-DEM plan is based on the following:

1.  Understanding the transient/dependent emotions that constitute the predominant mood of love at the workplace.
2.  Acknowledging the elements of love with respect to the three categories of relationships (peers, juniors, superiors).
3.  Applying the 5As framework to love at the workplace.

In Rati's case, a positive atmosphere led to constructive collaboration and achievement. As per the *Navrasa* (nine emotional moods) theory, the state of the *rasa* (mood) manifests due to the cause or trigger of the *vibhav* (emotion), the effect of the emotion is the *anubhava* and the transient/related emotions are the *vyabhichari*. While *rasas* denote the mood, these *bhavas* (associated with each *rasa*) create the mood through physical media—the brain, body or action.

The following table based on the arts, helps us classify the emotions connected with the dominant emotion of love/beauty/delight.

| Vibhav (Cause) | Sthahi Bhav (Dominant Emotion) | Anubhava (Experience) | Vyabhichari (Related Emotions) | Response | | |
|---|---|---|---|---|---|---|
| | *Shringar* | | | *Uttama* (high) | *Madhyama* (medium) | *Adhama* (low) |
| Actions/ Events leading to positive emotion | Love/ Beauty/ Delight | Warmth in behaviour | Pride, feeling of nurturing, respect, admiration, devotion, loyalty, aesthetic sentiment | Words of praise, smile, joy, | Pat on the back, a hug (if permitted culturally) | Physical display of affection where it may not be culturally appropriate |

## The Power of Workplace Chemistry

Like the much celebrated 'onscreen chemistry' of actor pairs and people passionately in love and physically attracted towards each other, there is immense power in workplace chemistry. So, what is this workplace chemistry? Co-workers sensing, anticipating, understanding and complimenting each other's skillsets, quirks and 'workplace needs'. The root of this workplace chemistry once again lies in mutual trust. Given the ease, comfort level and the non-verbal communication that is involved in work chemistry, the term 'office spouse' came into vogue few years ago. But 'office chemistry' does not involve any romantic relationship.

No doubt, office spouses like or love working with each other and like/love their co-worker as a person.

As the ancient Indian texts say, the beauty of the *Shringar Rasa* is in the 'tasting' rather than 'eating'.

Love (like all good things) could also be addictive. That is why one often finds people reluctant to change teams/colleagues/bosses.

Whenever a boss/subordinate relationship transcends the stage of being exclusively professional, it is most likely to evolve into a formal or informal mentoring relationship. The root of a mentoring relationship is the mentee's acknowledgment (primarily to oneself and then within the larger ecosystem) that there is something he/she is yet to learn and the potential mentor has the capability to provide that learning. If mentees do not demonstrate such humility, it is impossible to have a mentor–mentee relationship, especially at the workplace.

This is not to say that successful workplaces can only be built on the back of mentor–mentee relationships. It is possible to have a manager–individual contributor relationship based on mutual respect that is exclusively professional in nature and thus more transactional than emotional. Therefore, so many successful professionals never have a mentor or mentor anyone in their lives. Once again, this is a choice they have exercised.

Table 3.1 demonstrates the stages of a mentoring relationship. These stages are not static.

**Table 3.1**  Stages of a Mentoring Relationship

| | 1 | 2 | 3 | 4 |
|---|---|---|---|---|
| **Stage** | **Initiation** | **Cultivation** | **Separation** | **Redefinition** |
| Occurrences | Preparing, negotiating | More opportunities to interact, support, regular feedback | Mentee outgrows relationship | Relationship is supposed to settle as friendship of equality with the hierarchy removed |
| Mentee's emotion | Is my mentor right for me? | Enhanced importance of the relationship | Self-reliance, independence, assess value | I know this, what more can I learn? |
| Mentor's emotion | What is the goal of this interaction? Do I have buy-in? | Satisfaction that the mentee is learning | Prepare to move on | Opportunity for mentor to learn, become more self-aware |
| Bosses as mentors | Set context, build rapport, creating work as well as 'learning goals, establish' shared responsibilities and ground rules | Challenge assumptions, support learning | Break or close project | Celebrate achievement |

*Source:* Kram[1] (1985, 47–66).

In reality, when an emotional connect has been developed (which is natural), both parties may never move on completely. They may see less of each other but would always care for each other's happiness, joy. If the separation happens prematurely, the mentee would experience the feeling of abandonment. If it continues beyond the need felt by the mentee, it may feel like an oppressive relationship.

---

[1] Professor of Organizational Behaviour at Boston University School of Management, Kathy Kram has written several publications on mentoring.

How can you apply the 5A framework?

How could Rati have dealt with the extreme emotion of love? The answer is by applying the 5As framework.

| | | | |
|---|---|---|---|
| 1 | Acknowledge | I feel positive when I go to work. I like some of my colleagues more than I like others. In fact, I love some of them. So much so that we share 'work chemistry'. | I am feeling something. And the feeling is positive. It is 'love' in one of its varied forms. |
| 2 | Analyse | It will help to put into categories what I'm really feeling (see the nine emotional moods) and understand at least some of what happens in the brain. | I feel valued and trusted. I am now dependent on the people at my workplace (at least two of them) to make me feel good. |
| 3 | Accept | Love hurts. If you have an ecosystem where your workplace is more than a set of bodies performing tasks, there will be relationships and they hurt. | I have allowed my co-workers to touch my core. If they do not behave in the way I expect them to, it affects me much more than it would if they were just co-workers. |

(continued)

*(continued)*

| 4 | Administer | I will 'choose' my attitude. | I should be aware that having made the choice to be led by emotion, I am more vulnerable. I am aware of the effect my co-workers have on me and I have on them. |
| 5 | Act | I will 'follow' my plan. | At this moment, I believe there are more advantages of the emotional connect than disadvantages and I will continue to build these connects. |

# Reference

Kram, Kathy Kram. 1985. *Mentoring at Work*. Glenview, IL: Scott, Foresman and Company.

# Fear

*I learned that courage was not the absence of fear, but the triumph over it. The brave man is not he who does not feel afraid, but he who conquers that fear.*

—Nelson Mandela

As per our survey, of all people who left jobs due to emotional issues,

- 14 per cent left because fear was the emotion that made them leave the job.
- 15 per cent had leveraged fear to increase productivity.

## Depicting 'Fear' in the Arts

Dramatic depictions of fear will show a person cowering, as if shrinking (making himself/herself smaller) so as to be hidden from the attacking entity. The eyes are wide if the fear is coupled with shock of a sudden attack. The fists are closed tightly and if the attack is anticipated (like a blow or a storm/lightening), the eyes are tightly shut as if to protect one of the most sensitive parts of the body from harm.

At the workplace though, in order to keep up with the norms of work life, there is a fear of showing that one is afraid as well! Those who are afraid at work are unlikely to demonstrate such dramatic symptoms. Fear is more likely to surface as someone looking into someone else's computer through the corner of his/her eye!

## The Science Behind Fear

The physical manifestations of fear are mostly involuntary responses to scary stimuli. This would include trembling, sweating of palms, flushing of the skin, rapid heartbeat, fainting, dizziness, freezing of limbs and several others depending on the severity of the situation and pre-conditioning of the person who is afraid. The 'fear centre' or amygdala in the brain would depend on a person's prior experience of similar situations for the brain to interpret what the body should expect. For example, toddlers rarely demonstrate fear of heights, fire, water, insects or any other potentially dangerous situations as they simply do not have prior experience with the bad effects of these!

Managers create fear in the workplace to get work done. Leaders create trust in the workplace to work with teams to get work done. It is not possible for fear and trust to exist at the same time. When trust and fear have a face-off, fear will beat trust every time. A very simple way to understand if fear or trust dominates the workplace is to look at the 'Yes' and 'No' culture. Do all subordinates simple say a 'Yes' to their line manager or do you see them challenging their senior with the approach being taken? Trust will allow colleagues to challenge each other and fear will hold them back and just do what is needed to protect their jobs.

If your manager watches you like a vulture, who wants to know what you are working on and how it is going or you are worried about your being managed that way, it's fear that's holding you from reaching your potential at the workplace.

If you have a manager who doesn't watch over you like an eagle, doesn't investigate every minor task you are doing and doesn't have a daily meeting with you to just give an update on what you are doing that day, then it is highly likely that they are focused on the mission and trust that their team is on it. And your team will trust the leader.

Following are some examples of fear taking over a workplace in small instances that sometimes go unnoticed.

1.  **Timekeeping and fear of the system**
    An employee will be afraid of swiping in and out of office on time, so they don't get flagged for not

working their hours. Even if they never get flagged, their day starts with the fear of swiping in before 9 AM. Taxi drivers are typically self-employed and are on zero contracting hours. These contractors who are self-employed always have a constant fear of being watched by the system and getting booted out if they don't perform well.

2. **Castles in the cloud**

   This implies a business where employees feel they have been promised collaboration and communication from the management, but it never materializes. When fear takes over employees, when they are lured into buying the idea again and again, only to be disappointed, they are afraid of disappointment yet another time. This builds up fear even for new people joining in as they get inputs from the existing team.

3. **Sudden resignation**

   Sudden resignation of a high-performing employee or sometimes a senior leaving the business overnight can instil fear in the rest of the team as they used to look up to that one hard working person. Gossip, rumours and silence from the management team can instil fear in such proportion that others start getting restless and looking out for options too.

4. **Blame game**

   Fear will preside where there is a culture to blame another team or person for a project or process that has failed. Because of that fear, aggression and anger take over. An employee is not excited about making the project a success and instead is hoping that he/she will not mess it up. A salesperson will not be excited about exceeding his targets but will hope he will end up at least doing the minimum, simply because he is aware that he will be blamed for the poor sales, not the market, not the product.

5. **Redundancies**

   The 'R' word creates fear from the top to the bottom level at the workplace. Not knowing if you will have a job the next week creates doubts and is a fear that many time leads to an employee resigning anyways. Bad results followed by no salary increments can lead to gossip about redundancies as the next obvious step.

6. **White elephant**

   It's one thing to have awesome and inspiring mission and vision statements, and then there are conversations in hidden rooms that no one wants to hear about—employees talking about how it is the same every time and that they are not heard. There is an elephant in the room that needs to be addressed, but no one wants to look at it or talk about it. People have a fear of expressing the thought 'We know all about these great things, but do you know what we really go through?'

7. **Awards and rewards**

   If there is a culture of a numbers game where people are purely rewarded/promoted based on performance instead of performance and behaviour, there is fear. The numbers game takes over everything. Show me the numbers, and you get promoted. Show me average performance, and you will be booted out no matter how authentic you are.

8. **Leaders losing it**

   You know the moment when kids freeze when daddy gets angry and they know they have messed up big time. Imagine a leader having a similar go at this team, though for no reason. Fear sweeps like wildfire when a leader loses his/her mind and goes on a hunt blaming the team for everything. If the captain of the ship loses it, the sailors are bound to be drowning in fear, perhaps the ship as well.

9. **Meeting before the meeting**

   Have you ever had this strange feeling on why are we having a meeting before a meeting? It's a normal meeting, and your manager wants to have a meeting before the meeting. The meeting is not a prep check or a mentoring session. It's just a meeting to tell the manager we are all ready. Even worse is the case where the manager has given his subordinate the platform to present to the senior team but tells them what to say and what not to say. The subordinate will pretty much doubt and have a fear that the manager does not trust him/her with running the meeting.

10. **One-way talk**

    Leaders will merely be talking if they don't encourage instant feedback. For real communication, it must be a two-way game, not a one-way lane. A simple way to check is to note what kind of questions come up in the Q&A in open leadership sessions—are they hard-hitting open questions towards the management or fluffy and soft-ended questions or maybe none.

Fear at the workplace is more common than common cold in winter. We will always be fearful of something in the workplace all the time.

Here are some reasons why we feel fear in the workplace.

1.  **Fear of failure**

    The workplace is changing all the time; process, people, moods, targets, everything keeps changing. There is a massive fear of failure around jobs that have sales targets. Operational roles are afraid of failing in managing key performance indicators. The security guard will be fearful of being outsmarted by a robber who will breach security. Fear is always present; it's about how one manages it.

2.  **Fear of embarrassment**

    A very common fear is the fear of embarrassment. Being afraid to reply to an email that has seniors copied on it. Being afraid to ask a question in front of a team, let alone one to one, being afraid to call up and say you will be late as you must drop your kids at school, being afraid to ask for a pay rise— these are all indications of fear out of embarrassment.

Instead of thinking 'why should I embarrass myself at the workplace,' think 'Why "shouldn't" I embarrass myself at the workplace. What is the worst that could happen? Sometimes embarrassment opens up a new and stronger bond between the manager and teams.'

3. **Fear of the high performer**

Ever had a team where one person outperforms everyone else? It takes one person half the time to get the sales done or complete the process that others take more time on. Some of these other people have a fear of performing lower than the best ones. These people are normally seen slogging away on weekends and in the evenings to complete work while they look at the superhero who does it super quick.

This mostly happens when there is no consistent feedback from managers.

4. **Fear of rejection**

Fear of rejection goes one step ahead of fear of embarrassment. Put the same reason for fear of embarrassment and replace it with rejection. A person with this fear states 'I don't care if I get embarrassed, what if I get rejected?'

This fear of rejection holds back so many potential high performers from doing awesome stuff at work.

5. **Fear of change**

Organization structure change always takes employees by surprise. There is fear of where a person's role fits in the new structure. A fear of what happens when the new system is deployed. Fear of what will happen to the jobs when robots or AI take over.

Change brings uncertainty which pushes people out of their comfort zone. For example, the fear of Brexit and the changes it will bring had given cold feet to so many small entrepreneurs and big business too in the UK.

## The story of fear of the 'business update'

At a client site in the UK, Brexit was hitting the business hard, and the retail business was struggling. That year, there was no employee survey, nobody was saying anything from the leadership team. Fear was making its presence felt.

Then it happened. Everyone got an invitation for a 'Business Update'. On the day of some announcement, everyone was in, on time. There was silence and whispers, and people were talking about redundancies. Fear was even more visible.

The moment arrived. Everyone was gathered on the second floor; the CEO walked in. With a poker face, she read out word by word from a page. 'We haven't had a great year, and as a business, we need to do more. This is mostly down to external factors such as Brexit. For that reason, there will be no salary increments in the annual performance review.' Now everyone was more scared. They knew the next message would be to make some redundancies.

'In view of the same while we understand that not having salary increments is not the news you would want to hear. We are giving everyone additional five paid holidays this year.' The emotion in the room shifted from fear to confusion. Some were happy about the five holidays. That was it. The CEO left; there was no formal email to confirm the announcement.

And then there was silence again regarding further updates. The leadership team went quiet again. Everyone started gossiping and talking again. Maybe there will be redundancies. And then, the flood of resignations started coming through. The silence allowed fear to take over trust and people were leaving by the dozen.

The whole head office had refurbished the building to make space for more desks as it was getting full, and now there were empty desks on every floor.

## The story of the 'fear of exceptions and fear of decisions'

As per standard practice, no insurance company would pay the insured sum if the death of a policyholder was a suicide. A major insurance company as an exception respected a policyholder although it was known that he had killed himself of fear. It wasn't fear of banks chasing for money or some emotional trauma. It was a decision he was aware of. He was a soldier who was on a secret mission across the enemy border and was found out by the enemy as he jumped off an aircraft and was landing with the help of a chute.

When he realised he was identified by the enemy on the ground, he had to make a decision. He noticed that no one was firing at him, with the intention to catch him alive to interrogate him. He could be tortured to get sensitive information or used as a tool to exchange with terrorists captured by his country. He made a conscious decision of killing himself before he hit the ground. Technically, he did commit suicide, but it was to protect the secrets of his nation and perhaps to avoid the enemy coaxing any information out of him. Fear is bad. It is natural, what is needed is to channelize it the right way. He fought his fear, died but won the battle.

## The story of being reprimanded for breaking a rule

Simon Sinek in his Ted talk on 'why good leaders make you feel safe' says: 'I was on a flight and I was a witness to an incident where a passenger attempted to board before their number was called, and I watched the gate agent treat this man like he had broken the law, like a criminal. He was yelled at for attempting to board one group too soon. So, I said something. I said, "Why do you have to treat us like cattle? Why can't you treat us like human beings?" And this is exactly what she said to me: She said, "Sir if I don't follow the rules, I could get in trouble or lose my job." All she was telling me is that she doesn't feel safe. All she was telling me is that she doesn't trust her leaders. The reason we like flying Southwest Airlines is not because they necessarily hire better people. It's because they don't fear their leaders.'[1]

## The story of Project Bluebird: Fear of the client

13 February 2015, London.

At 9.45 AM on a chilly Friday the 13th, the boardroom at the Airborne Publishing headquarters in Central London looked empty. Notepad and pen in place, her presentation up and running, Maya, Programme Manager, GlobalTech UK, was all set for the programme review with the client—Airborne. Across the grand boardroom table sat Mandeep, Head of GlobalTech, Europe.

---

[1] https://www.ted.com/talks/simon_sinek_why_good_leaders_make_you_feel_safe

Maya said, 'I told you last week Mandeep. Since Walter replaced Chris, my instinct says something is very wrong. Paula, Alison (Maya's manager at the customer Airborne end), Walter are sitting outside the boardroom. They greeted me warmly like they always do, but refused to come into the room saying they are waiting for the CTO and MD.'

'Strange!' muttered Mandeep just as the Airborne contingent led by CTO Mark Williams and MD Theo Dawson walked in.

Handshakes, hellos and a futile attempt to arrange for GlobalTech's UK Sales head Raj (Maya's manager at her own employer GlobalTech end) to be included on the conference call, CTO Mark got straight to the point, 'We are aware Mandeep, since you stepped in, every attempt has been made to set things right, including bringing on board the best of programme management people (nod at Maya). These efforts have been well appreciated. However, I'm sorry but Airborne cannot afford to risk software code review failure again. I'm afraid the software code being delivered is of poor quality and I understand the last code review turned out to be a training session for my team to train yours. Given the time our development team is spending doing that, they have decided to finish Project Bluebird writing code themselves.'

Maya was stunned by the comment on the sweeping 'simplistic senior management version' (The higher up people go, the more simplified they like information to be [Isenberg 1984]) of the code review saga and blatant strategic misrepresentation (Machiavelli 1513) by Airborne software development head Ashfaque leading to Mark's comment on 'training'.

Though Maya was not a software programmer, she had facilitated the last two intercontinental code reviews via video conference. What had transpired during the last one few days ago was a spirited discussion between Airborne's senior developer Gareth (Ashfaque's reportee) and GlobalTech's competent but rather outspoken solution architect Dharmendra on two different methods of organizing backend software code. It had taken concerted effort to organize for video conferencing software on Gareth's desktop (only senior staff at Airborne had laptops) to facilitate 'sharing screens' and encourage Gareth and Dharmendra to interact on video calls instead of lengthy technical email discussions that triggered senior management comments on 'time wastage and too much guidance from Airborne'. Appreciating Gareth's hearing disability and Dharmendra's thick North Indian accent, Maya suggested Dharmendra visually demonstrate his suggestion using a drawing board. At the end of the code review, Maya asked Gareth his verdict.

'I'm supposed to report this to my manager,' he said shuffling his feet. 'Ashfaque will let Alison know and she will convey it to you.'

Over the years, Maya had learnt to veil her frustration with red tape (Indian and English—there was no cultural difference on that one, thanks colonization!) (Meyer 2014b).

Since the past 7 weeks, from across the aisle in the London office, Gareth had observed Maya toil 14 hours a day to make this work. Her response to his wary, clinical answers had been warmth and understanding alone and a genuine plea for help. As he stepped out of the room, Gareth said,

'Maya, this code review was so much better than the previous ones. We're getting there!'

Instead of narrating this code review episode to the dignified chill in the room, Maya looked at Mandeep. 'I'm sorry it has ended this way,' said Mandeep to the group.

MD Theo Dawson added, 'I'm sorry that the two people who made every attempt to make this work, need to bear this news. You tried hard but came in too late into the project.'

Maya's presentation would have defended these points. But it was too late. The decision had been made. For the first time in her 8 weeks at the Bluebird programme, she said nothing.

Handshakes, nods and exit. CTO Mark's wise blue eyes bore into Maya's stricken black ones as he said,

'Don't take this personally Maya. It is not about project management. You were setting everything right there. It was about people's capability to write software code.'

As Maya and Mandeep stepped out into the busy London street, Mandeep said,

'In my 30-year career in outsourcing, this is just the second time I've been in such a meeting. And both times, I've been told I stepped in too late. I didn't want to argue about the code and trigger litigation.' And just like that, Maya lost her contract, her job, the income she was depending on—all because of the continued 'fear' of the 'client'.

# Background

Mandeep and Maya had worked together eight years ago at another Indian software company. Maya had worked in India during the major part of her career and then with a London-based corporation. Mandeep had grown up in the UK and would wryly describe himself as 'the only non-Indian in an Indian company' (Global cosmopolitan-Meyer 2014b).

After Mandeep joined GlobalTech as Europe Head three months ago, the burning issue in his otherwise successful portfolio was Airborne's IT outsourcing programme Bluebird being delivered by GlobalTech's development team based in New Delhi, India. The project manager position had been vacant for weeks, the software code reviews were failing and Airborne was threatening to terminate the contract. Mandeep then approached Maya, offering her the challenge of a turnaround.

## The Stakeholders

Maya made a pre-Christmas start at Airborne's UK office due to the sense of urgency that prevailed and worked from UK at Indian timelines (Indian work culture is characterized by absent work-life balance [Turner, Lingard and Francis 2009]). She spent the Christmas weeks 'relationship mapping' (Qi 2003) setting up individual video calls with each stakeholder in India. She reached out individually to every stakeholder in the Airborne team. They were wary but candid and professional, clearly conveying that they were willing to help make this work. Maya had been specifically told by Chris and had an email from Ashfaque saying he was now 'concentrating on other essential projects' and that Alan would be the point of contact for Bluebird. He was never a part of any of the official Bluebird emails/meetings.

A week before Bluebird terminated, Ashfaque and Alison's boss Chris was replaced by Walter. In a meeting with Walter, Alison and Maya, Ashfaque made a passionate speech about Bluebird standing on software code that was a pile of dust and the roof would collapse over Airborne any time. Realizing that Ashfaque was back into the project and heavily influencing his new boss, Maya sought Ashfaque's advice on the code review saga. The meeting ended in five minutes. Ashfaque stated,

'There is nothing to be done. Your Delhi team does not know how to write code.'

To understand what went wrong, let's look at some of the pertinent Airborne stakeholder statements to Maya when she started at Bluebird.

'If we were to spend so long in dealing with multiple queries from GlobalTech India, we could have just done it ourselves!' (Paula and Mark)

'They are working hard. But we don't have the confidence in their process or their understanding of Agile.' (Chris Jones)

'The software code quality we expect is of high standards. They have failed our reviews.' (Alison)

Maya focused on establishing a change in the 'visual performing space' and management and accounting controls (Quattrone and Busco 2014) supplementing the call with a daily tracker that used the standard British way of communication, effectively reducing the cultural gap (Meyer 2014a). Concerted effort in the areas providing dry and wet data (Goguen 1992), addressing all aspects of Galbraith's star within Bluebird's temporary organization (Wiley) succeeded.

After the software demo to the Airborne team in Week 3, Maya was overwhelmed by the appreciation from all the stakeholders for setting Bluebird on track.

'I trust you implicitly. With your professionalism and passion, our calls with the team in India have been streamlined—it is fantastic!' said an exuberated Alison, Airborne's Project Manager and Maya's boss. In week 4, Airborne PMO was advising Maya and Alison to report Bluebird as green, outside the danger zone! 'But for the software code review, it would have!' said Alison.

And yet, the project failed.

Failure reasons included Airborne's own internal baggage, Maya's own overconfidence and lack of technical knowledge and technical inability (contextual intelligence). A fundamental factor—'customer as competition' (Porter 2008)—overrules.

But the biggest reason for the failure of this project was the fear cascade:

- Fear of losing the project—Maya, Mandeep, Raj and everyone at GlobalTech
- Fear of displeasing a customer—though it was amply evident that Ashfaque did not 'want' the project to succeed and the verdict of 'code failure' was evident even before the code review, fear of displeasing the customer stopped Maya from stating this upfront to Alison and the others at Airborne.

When Maya did suggest a blind, external code review, it was too late and all was lost.

- Hidden even deeper is the root cause of Ashfaque's resistance to GlobalTech—he was alarmed to see Project Bluebird taking shape and the needle moving from red to amber to green soon. The success of this project would mean the reduced importance of his team at Airborne. And if the success story continued, it could potentially mean a job loss for him and his team. Whether real or imagined, this fear was why the project really failed!

The story proves that if the white swans are acknowledged and addressed, the black swan in the form of strategic mis-representation by a stakeholder exerting covert influence can be extremely powerful (Taleb 2010).

Porter's five forces can only be used as the starting point. There are other non-market forces including the cultural/administrative/geographical/economic (CAGE/GRACE; Ghemawat 2001, 2017) distance. The explicitly stated (white swan) non-market issues could be explained by the distance between India and the UK. This was compounded by Airborne's customer bargaining power (Porter 2008) and GlobalTech's overt willingness to accommodate every request in order to retain the project that had taken its UK sales head (Maya's boss Raj) two years of sales effort to win.

## Situation Diagnosis

Maya's overall assessment on arrival was that the Airborne PM (Alison) and development representative (Alan) were micro-managing Bluebird and were also blaming GlobalTech for taking up too much of their time! The CAGE distance was not in the Indian team's ability to speak in English during the daily 'Stand-up video calls' but how they would communicate (Pattnaik 2009). As London-based Magic PM Nuno said to Maya about the Indian stereotype (Meyer 2014b),

'When Indians speak, they just Go go go!'

Apart from her day job as PM, Maya played the role of interpreting the Indian 'Go go' for the British audience used to a binding structure stating what they will state and then stating and summarizing it.

*What does a flat world look like?* Professionalism, no discrimination based on diversity in race/gender/disability/location of work, etc., opinion, political correctness, personal space.

*Flatness indicators:* acceptance of modern concepts such as flexible working, audio/video conference calls instead of face-to-face meetings, usage of electronic modes of communication, reduced red tape, timeliness (Ghemawat 2009).

If the world is flat (Friedman 2009), the flatness quotient for both UK and India should have been high. While Friedman's argument has its merits, and is true to a large extent, in reality, organizations, countries and people are in different stages of the flatness.

Maya should have recognized that though Ashfaque had been formally asked to stay away from the programme, his covert influence would continue its adverse impact on the single area where she had least control and no expertise—software code review.

When she did realize that the Ashfaque factor had raised its head after Walter's arrival and she did raise the issue of strategic misrepresentation to Alison and Walter, it was too late. Nobody was in a mood to listen. She could have approached Paula and Mark directly, but would they have listened?

The answer lies in the 'informal' conversation between Alison and Maya days after the MP had been terminated.

Alison, 'Your professionalism and passion has been fantastic. I know, if you could write that software code, you would have!'

Maya 'Thanks Alison. Could I make an informal suggestion for future projects?'

Both organizations have suffered as the project managers did not have a technical background. The process henceforth could include an 'external technical review' conducted 'blind' by a neutral party with no stake in the success or failure of the project.

'I am not discounting any of this Maya. Will implement this in future!'

## The Solution Matrix

Look at the following table and identify the pattern of your feelings when you are afraid:

| Vibhav (Cause) | Sthahi Bhav (Dominant Emotion) | Anubhava (Experience) | Vyabhichari (Related Emotions) | Response |
|---|---|---|---|---|
| Fear | Fight or flight behaviour | Goose bumps, increased heartbeat, quick shallow breath and seating, slowdown of body functions not needed, sharpening of functions needed to survive, butterflies in stomach | Embarrassment, loss, overwhelming joy | Weakens our immune system, causes cardiovascular damage, ulcers and irritable bowel syndrome, premature death.  Affects long-term memories, fatigue, clinical depression |

## Applying the 'A' framework:

| 1 | Acknowledge | Next time you hesitate to do something you know you should have, don't ignore it. Tell yourself it is fear that is holding you back, trying to make its way through your body and mind. It's as easy as telling yourself 'I am feeling fear right now,' aloud! |
|---|---|---|
| 2 | Analyse | So, you know you are feeling fear, but what next? What exactly are you afraid of? What is the worst thing that will happen if you were to do what you want to do? Analyse it; feel it deep. Notice what is happening to your body and mind. Where are you feeling it the most? And remind yourself that fear is as common as the common cold and you can control it. There are so many people who have, are and will be feeling the same fear. So, you are not alone, and you will be okay. |
| 3 | Accept | Take a piece of paper and write down your fear on it. Just say it out loud to someone. This is where, in the fight or flight mode, you have decided to accept the fear. Get it out of your system and express its presence. |
| 4 | Administer | How do you administer the solution for fear—doing what scares you and then waiting to see the results? There are some questions further in a section that will help you administer the right solution when faced with fear. Administering will pose the first question—'Do we choose fight or flight?' and whatever the response is, challenge it. If the mind says fight, think of a reason to run away. If it is flight, think of a reason to fight. Trying to think the opposite of what the instinct tells you helps you slow down the thought process and list out more options. |
| 5 | Act | To act while feeling fear takes courage. Courage needs confidence. Confidence is a by-product of an act once done. Feel the fear and just do it anyways. And once you do it, the fear is gone. Run it again in your mind to register how you felt so your mind and body are in sync with the event. |

# Tools/Tips/Worksheets

There is no good or bad fear. There is just fear. Feel the fear and do it anyways. Do what? Do this:

- **Name your fear**
  Being able to voice out and give a name to your fear takes a lot of guts. You could be a project manager who fears to deal with a specific stakeholder. Speaking it out to someone you can talk to will help you release the pressure and focus on the issue and not the person. Again, don't speak out of defence, speak out the truth. 'I fear….' instead of 'I am trying to deal with….' The difference is simply if you haven't let your fear out yet, you cannot focus on dealing with it.

- **Making it fear as usual**
  When the leadership team says, 'The market is tough, but we are in business as usual mode,' it rings alarms. The first thought is that it will go wrong at some point. How about if fear had a usual mode? The leader inside you tells your emotions, 'I know we are feeling un-comfortable but it is fear as usual and nothing new.' Being aware and knowing that it is a usual fear and nothing new reduces the intensity behind it.

  When my 3-year-old child plays the 'monster' game with me, he will act scared, but he knows it's just a game and just daddy acting like a monster. When it comes to bedtime, he does not want to sleep in the dark. For him, playtime is fear, as usual, fun and games, so it does not scare him. But bedtime is serious, and sleeping is a task and the thought of a monster in the dark spooks him. Even the CEO who is trying to scare you by using the redundancy word fears his stakeholders and business performance. The CEO is probably as scared as you are. If you are a leader and feel that someone in your team is feeling scared of something at the workplace, suggest you share your story of what you fear rather than trying to encourage them with inspiring words. Once they know that you too are scared, they will start thinking in fear as usual mode.

- **Help me**

  Seeking help is okay. Talking to someone about our fear is okay. Being afraid of fear is fine. There are so many users who get so scared of system changes in their business. They will shout and cry about how awful the new software is. There could be some in there who don't really hate the software but fear the new interface. This was true when so many businesses were moving from a black and green DOS screen to flashy Windows 95 screen.

  Instead of moaning about that new printer, it is okay to face the fear of embarrassment and say, 'I don't know how to use these modern touchscreen printers, can someone help me. I don't like how they are, and I hate them.'

- **Lean into fear**

  What is the worst that could happen? Unless you are on the border in a war zone, what is the worst that could happen? Thinking of the worst-case scenario sometimes allows you to lean into your fear. Redundancy is a scary word. It is a scary announcement to listen to. But what is the worst-case scenario?

You could be made redundant or not. If not, it's okay, if yes, then you could find a new job instantly or you will not. If you don't, you could find a job before running out of your cash flow or not. If you do run out of cash flow, you could then think of borrowing money from some source to survive till you find a job. Or maybe just get an income protection insurance if it is money that bothers you. There is always a worst-case scenario but how scary can it be? The fear, in this case, was not redundancy but lack of funds for losing the job.

- **Dating with fear**
  Focus on one thing at a time. And one of it should be dating with fear. Allocate time in the day to focus on fear—a 15-minute routine to make a list of your present fear and to think and look at different perspectives in that time. To get an edge, think of a fear that may hit you in future. A presentation you must do is scaring you. Spend 15 minutes thinking and look at the fear of presenting from a different perspective. Some relevant questions you can use have been mentioned further in the chapter.

- **Fear is as common as common cold**
  What if you told yourself, again and again, that fear is okay? It is normal. It is as common as the common cold. What if you told yourself if you don't feel the fear, you are not pushing yourself to grow? When fear becomes a common event in mind not as something to deal with forever, but as 'fear as usual' it becomes easier to deal with the initial impact.

- **Confirm and clear expectations**
  Be clear on what you expect. Seek answers with the right questions till you know what is expected. Having clarity both ways on what is expected in the form of deliverables removes performance fear.

## Question Quotient

The right questions don't usually lead to right answers. They lead to silence and space where the client can view their fear from all perspectives and get to know it better. Following are some questions you can use:

1.  What would it mean if you were not scared about that?
    Whenever you feel a sense of fear, ask yourself 'What would it mean if I wasn't scared of it?' You have been told about a possible redundancy, or a pay-cut, or performance issues. What if you told yourself, I will do anything but be scared? What would come to your mind? Stop reading or listening to this book right now and think about the last time you were scared at the workplace and play with the same question when the fear initially sets in.

2.  Are you always scared, even when…?
    Fear is often an internal struggle and sometimes has less to do anything with the outside. Fearing the CEO, for example—some people get nervous when their senior executives are around or when their manager who has been working with them for years shouts at them randomly. Initially, there is fear, as to why is this person whom I have been working

with for so many years going mad at me. Then there will be a fight or flight approach where you either quit or argue with your manager. Ask yourself 'Am I also scared when I am meeting him/her outside office' or when he appreciates me for what I have done or would I still be scared if someone else is shouting in the same tone or may be at a different workplace?

3.  Teach me how to get filled with fear like you.
    Learning the process of how fear grows inside you will help you identify it earlier in the process and not let it grow. This is useful in the acknowledging stage. How would you write down the process of feeling fear if it was to be taught to someone? Write the steps on a paper. For example,

    - Feeling breathless around the lungs, hollowness
    - Trembling fingers
    - Sweating
    - Not being able to put words together

    Once you know the recipe for cooking fear, you can cook it the way you want. Keep it raw or leave it aside to simmer as you know it won't materialize.

4.  How will this fear impact everything else around you?
    Fear at the workplace is often not about being scared for yourself. If there are rumours about possible redundancies or a tough manager, different men and women will look at it differently.

    For example, redundancies will scare a person with family responsibilities more than a single person.

Three simple words 'paying the bills!' Paying the bills, mortgage, school fees helps face fear in a different way. Listening to utter nonsense from your line manager will be better than not having the money to pay the family bills. Both fears coexist—fear of a bad manager and fear of leaving the job and not having money to pay the bills. For one type of fear, we choose the flight and for the other we choose to fight. Think of the wider elements around you that will be impacted if you decided to be scared and once you accept you are scared, you can then make an informed decision.

5. What happens when you imagine yourself being scared?
   Dive deep inside your mind. What is happening inside your body when you are imagining yourself getting scared when you are feeling the fear and holding it? Where do your muscles get tense? What happens inside your mind? What thoughts are coming to your mind? Can you slow them down? Can you speed them up? Can you rewind, pause and replay? This is one way to feel the fear, by playing with it.

6. What is the worst thing for you about being scared?
   This is not about what will happen if your fear did come true. It is, what is the worst thing about you being scared right now? Is it that you are aware that you have had this experience before several times and the worst thing is, it manages to scare you every time? Or that every time it happens you make a wrong decision?

7.  What will you do when you become scared enough? What is the worst-case scenario? How long will you choose to feel and let your fear be within you? What will happen when that fear starts suffocating you? What will you do when you have had enough of the fear? Fight or flight? And who will you become? Will you become your favourite superhero and fight it out or will you ignore as if nothing is happening?

8.  Who and what specifically?
    Sometimes fear kicks in and takes you by surprise. Imagine sitting at your desk, working and you happen to see two office colleagues talking in whispers. The mind starts to build up stories. What are they talking about? Do they know something that I don't? And the stories start to build up in our mind. To break this pattern, asking the question who and what specifically will help clear the illusion, if any. Remember the example earlier about fear of losing. Who are you specifically scared of—the person who said something to you? Or not the person, maybe what he/she said scares you. Maybe not what he/she said, it may be the tone and timing of it. Or maybe, none of the above and it was the place where they said it. This question helps eliminate irrational fear and focus on the real issue at hand.

9.  How do you know when to get scared?
    What are the early signs of fear? When do you know it's time to get scared? Do you wait for few seconds before hitting the fear button or do you just go all in and start with fear leaving no time to understand the

reality? What triggers fear in you—place where you are, your body language, the person you are speaking to or something about the person?

Use the following template to play with your fear:

| What type of fear is it? | Describe the event in few lines | Have you had a similar experience in the past? | Will you fight or flight? Write the steps of action to take |
|---|---|---|---|
| Failure | | | |
| Embarrassment | | | |
| Comparison with high performers | | | |
| Change | | | |
| Rejection | | | |

A workplace is dynamic where change is constant—downsizing, upsizing, success, failure, IT problems, new software, new leaders, market speculation and so on. These events trigger emotions in people and fear is one of them. While leaders may or may not try and do what they can to eliminate the negative emotions, it's up to an individual to manage theirs. Accepting and acting on the fear is beneficial at all levels. Any workplace where fear is managed properly sees high turnover, less unscheduled leaves, less resignations and a positive outlook in the workplace and outside in the marketplace!

*Fear and courage are brothers.*—Proverb

# References

Friedman, Thomas. 2009. *The World Is Flat*. Yale University. Uploaded April 29, 2009, Available at: http://www.youtube.com/watch?v=53v LQnuV9FY (accessed on 9 January 2015).

Ghemawat, P. 2001. 'Distance Still Matters: The Hard Reality of Global Expansion.' *Harvard Business Review* 79(8): 137–47.

———. 2009. 'Why the World Isn't Flat.' October 14. Available at: https://foreignpolicy.com/2009/10/14/why-the-world-isnt-flat

———. 2017. *The Laws of Globalization*. Cambridge: Cambridge University Press.

Ghemawat, P., and P. Mathews. 2008. 'The Globalization of CEMEX.' *Harvard Business School Case* No. 9-701-017.

Goguen, J. 1992. 'The Dry and the Wet.' In *Information Systems Concepts: Proceedings of IFIP Working Group 8.1 Conference*. Amsterdam: North-Holland Publishing.

Isenberg, D. 1984. 'How Senior Managers Think.' *Harvard Business Review* 62 (6): 81–90.

Machiavelli, N. 1513. 'How Flatterers Should Be Avoided.' Chapter 23. In *The Prince*. Translated by W. K. Marriott. Available at: http://www.gutenberg.org/files/1232/1232-h/1232- h.htm#2HCH0023

Meyer, E. 2014a. *The Culture Map: Breaking Through the Invisible Boundaries of Global Business*. New York: PublicAffairs.

———. 2014b. 'Navigating the Cultural Minefield.' *Harvard Business Review* 92 (5): 119–23.

Pattnaik, D. 2009. 'East Meets West—The Myths that Mystify.' TED Talk. Available at: https://www.ted.com/talks/devdutt_pattanaik/transcript?language=en

Porter, M. 2008. 'The Five Competitive Forces That Shape Strategy.' *Harvard Business Review* 86 (1): 78–93. Reprint No. R0801E.

Quattrone, P. and Busco, C. 2014. 'Exploring How the Balanced Scorecard Engages and Unfolds: Articulating the Visual Power of Accounting Inscriptions.' *Contemporary Accounting Research* 32 (3): 1236–62.

Taleb, N. 2010. *The Black Swan: The Impact of the Highly Improbable*. 2nd ed. London: Penguin. ('Prologue', Chapters 1–3 and 10 'The Scandal of Prediction', pp. xvii–xxviii, pp. 1–37 and pp. 137–64.)

Tang Qi. 2003, July–August. 'Relationship Mapping.' *China Business Review* 30 (4): 28–30.

Turner, M., H. Lingard, and V. Francis. 2009. 'Work-life Balance: An Exploratory Study of Supports and Barriers in a Construction Project.' *International Journal of Managing Projects in Business* 2 (1): 94–111.

# Courage

*Success is not final, failure is not fatal: It is the
courage to continue that counts.*
    —Winston S. Churchill

# The Manifestation of Courage at the Workplace

The survey revealed the following results. Out of the individuals surveyed,

- 64 per cent used or leveraged emotions at work to improve productivity.
- 23 per cent used or leveraged heroism/courage to improve the pace or quality of their work.

## Depicting 'Heroism/Courage' in the Arts

In the traditional depictions of valour/courage in dance or drama, the protagonist is male, proficient in the martial arts and the legends revolve around this person's acts of bravery, vanquishing an enemy using his physical strength. So, in Hindu mythology quite similar to Greek mythology, one finds the most common imagery around courage manifest in the legends of the 'Ideal King' Rama killing the mighty, multi-faceted Ravan or the precocious child Krishna overpowering the Kalia snake.

The predominant emotional mood of courage (*veera* as defined in the Indian arts) has several transitionary/temporary emotions associated with it. In Indian classical dance or theatre, the expression of 'courage' is usually depicted with a calm but bold expression, the eyes focused on a single point in the audience, the lips very slightly upturned in a smile of satisfaction that achievement brings, the shoulders pulled back, torso erect and the hands holding the weapon that was used to vanquish the enemy. The body language depicting control over the situation is of prime importance as the core of courage is to have looked the problem in the eye, taken charge of the situation and having overcome the challenge.

## 'Heroism/Courage' in Science

The word 'hormone' was derived from the Greek word *hormao* meaning to arouse or put into quick motion. It was introduced in 1905 by a British physiologist, Professor Ernest Starling (Henderson 2005).

The two hormones associated with courage are oxytocin and testosterone.

Oxytocin is often defined as the 'courage hormone' given that it defends the body against stress hormones like cortisol. When this hormone is activated, it is supposed to have stimulated actions that activate trust, empathy, compassion and similar other emotions that are important to us, and diminish fear.[1]

Among the characteristics of testosterone (Crenshaw 1997) are that men have it more than 20–40 times more than women, it works as an anti-depressant in both genders, it increases assertiveness and self-confidence and is higher than usual in career women.

According to MedlinePlus,[2] the National Institutes of Health's website, normal testosterone levels vary in both males and females. For males, the range is between 300 and 1,000 ng/dl (nanograms per decilitre). For females, the range is between 15 and 70 ng/dl. Some of us tend to be 'high-T'

---

[1] https://www.scientificamerican.com/article/can-fear-be-erased/

[2] https://www.nih.gov/news-events/nih-research-matters/understanding-how-testosterone-affects-men (accessed on 22 June 2018).

type people, others tend to be 'low-T' type people, and most of us are somewhere in between.

According to Dr Dabbs, high-T and low-T are opposing strategies, one based on dominance and the other on cooperation (Dabbs and Dabbs 2000).

Dabbs, in fact, found that married men are lower in testosterone than single men and that testosterone levels drop when men get married and go up when they get divorced. He also found that men have higher levels of prolactin and lower levels of testosterone immediately after they become fathers.

These facts raise an important and interesting nuance about modern-day leadership which values cooperation more than dictatorship, and emphasize that women are better equipped to deal with leadership challenges today than when leadership personas were more dictatorial in nature (Tardanico 2013).

## Depicting 'Courage' at the Workplace

The demonstration of courage at the workplace is often a culmination of negative events/emotions such as anger and fear that demand a positive response. The events that demonstrate courage then could often be a combination of three positive emotions:

1.  Humour—Even in the midst of a crisis, it keeps the atmosphere light.
2.  Love/Delight ensures alignment towards the cause.
3.  Wonder—the unshakable belief that the miracle you wish to create is on its way.

## Courage at the workplace—Andrea's story

March 2017, Gurugram, National Capital Region (NCR), India.

As the helm of Sunbeam Children's hospital, Andrea had her work cut out. In the first hour of her arrival, she met her top team, her direct reportees—Parul, Burjor and Sadia—and the support team heads—Piali and Nitin. Back in Gurugram after a decade, Andrea had taken the (what others termed 'courageous') decision of moving back to what could easily be termed as one of India's most notorious places to live and work in.

When she looked out of the window, the Gurgaon she had left behind a decade ago with its sole 5-star hotel, pretty bungalows, small markets and modest homes was nowhere to be seen. Today's view had glass frontier high rises, massive hoardings and the back office of the world. Everything outside seemed new. But in the boardroom, that she was seated in, it wasn't all that new. Well, she had never met Piali, Nitin and Sadia before. Burjor had been a medical intern at the hospital she worked in a decade ago and Parul—well—she could not remember a time when she did not know Parul. What was new for the two people she did know, was the fact that they were to now be part of her team. As the hospital's trustee Dr Raheja introduced Andrea, there were broad smiles all round—all seemed to go well, at least for now!

The scorching heat of the North Indian summer, the dusty streets, the alarming increase in road traffic, the recurring news items on safety concerns in the NCR—what generally bothers people who have lived elsewhere—seemed miniscule to Andrea when she weighed these against the cause she was here for—children's health! A significant number of cases of child asthma (a result of the extreme weather conditions and the dismal record on air pollution), childhood obesity manifest due to the opulent sedentary lifestyles of the novae riche and the malnutrition among the infants in neighbouring villages—there was just so much to be done! Andrea swung into action to attack the first of the problems faced by the hospital— the shortage of junior doctors, nurses and ward staff. The recruitment issues gradually sorted, Andrea then went on to work with the fund-raising team for research grants.

On the surface, everything seemed fine. It was such a pleasure for Andrea to see how Burjor had evolved into a competent surgeon. When Piali launched the internal development programme for ward staff, nurses and junior doctors to upskill themselves, Burjor stood up and addressed the entire staff of Sunbeam,

'I am proud to say that when I worked with Andrea 10 years ago, I availed of the learning opportunities presented by such programmes. These are voluntary programmes and I remember as a 22-year-old, spending time beyond my work hours to be around other departments and learn. Do avail of this learning, it will help you grow in your career!' beamed Burjor.

Sadia and her team of nurses always maintained the decorum of a professional atmosphere and Parul—well—on the surface there were smiles all around. But what really happened in the realm of research, Andrea never knew for Parul would never let her know. Emails would go around the hospital, at conferences across the country and back and despite repeated requests Andrea would never be copied. Paediatrician conferences happened in the neighbouring state and Sunbeam did not feature even in the invitee list.

Funded by a charity and run by trustees, Andrea's mandate included raising certain level of funds, producing a certain number and quality of research papers and ensuring that path-breaking surgical procedures were performed in the hospital. As Andrea and Nitin sat down to map the hospital's performance against each of these criteria, it was shocking to see what emerged—the huge gap in expected versus actual funding and the massive expense bill way above budget.

To add to that was the shortfall of research papers committed to a medical journal for publication.

October 2018.

As the head of the organization, Andrea stood up to present her dismal statistics at board meetings, month after month with no visibility or control over how she would stem the tide. The monthly meetings would bring palpitations prior, deep insult during and frustration at her helplessness after the meetings.

It was during this period that the trustees floated a plan to start a chain of specialized diagnostic centres across the country. Dr Raheja recommended a role change for Parul as CEO of the Diagnostic centres' chain. When he asked Andrea when the handover should be, she promptly replied, 'If it is to happen, please do it immediately. If I am to take responsibility for everything that happens under this roof and bear the flak for everything that goes wrong, let me at least know what is going wrong and why,' she replied.

Within days, Parul moved over to assume her role as head of the new diagnostics' division. A chapter was closed, so thought Andrea and how wrong she was. The degeneration of what was to be one of her worst experiences as a leader had just begun.

A popular website where current and past employees could anonymously post reviews suddenly got active after eight months of silence. Personal attacks on Andrea, her work, the trustees, the 'war' among her direct reportees and versions of what someone somewhere who never had the courage to say or write found its way on this public forum empowered by anonymity.

A shocked Andrea reacted emotionally—sad that the children she had come to serve had been sidelined, sad that the teams she had tried to build and nurture had chinks where lies predominated and angry that the perpetuators of the vilification campaign were still blooming in the caustic atmosphere that had permeated the workplace. The gossip mongers were having a field day and Andrea was at the edge of disgust.

But even now, the worst had not come. In early August, Burjor had put in his papers citing personal reasons. He said he was willing to stay on for another six months in the interest of the long queue of children waiting for specialized surgery and the faith of corporate donors who had trusted Sunbeam with quality intervention and care. Though they had not been in touch in the interim years, over her months at Sunbeam, Andrea had thought she and Burjor had developed a warm relationship. When the time came for Burjor's departure, she wrote out a laudatory email, conducted a meeting with Burjor's team of doctors, right down to the junior-most interns and spoke about Burjor's phenomenal career growth in glorious terms.

December 2017.

In her email to all of Burjor's direct reportees and Sunbeam's management team, Andrea had mentioned that Burjor's responsibility will be shared by Sean, an upcoming surgeon, and Rani who had been handling surgical procedures with Burjor for the past few months. Burjor had mentioned to Andrea in passing that he had full faith in Rani's capability as he had groomed her. He also mentioned that Sean had a long way to go before he could handle a surgical department on his own.

Suddenly, during a progress review meeting with Dr Raheja, Burjor stated that Sean was not showing any interest, passion or desire to learn from him, and giving him any aspect of the surgical department to run was a sure recipe for disaster.

Andrea had recruited Sean and had been grooming him for the past few months to take on responsible roles. She and Dr Raheja had chosen Sean over all the external candidates they had evaluated. Given the criticality of the surgery division, they knew they could not afford to have anyone in the role of Head Surgeon who was not committed or passionate about the cause and excellent at his work. They decided to begin their search for a Head Surgeon all over again.

Andrea called Sean in the room and said, with pain in her heart but a professional look,

'Sean, I think you should stick to your previous role. Looks like the surgery position does not excite you and you have not been sticking to the handover schedule. I'm sad but I guess this is good for Sunbeam and our patients.' Sean walked away, angry, dejected, let down, contemplating whether to still serve the hospital that had propped him up and then let him down.

A few hours later, Andrea and Sean met again with the purpose of Andrea trying to pacify Sean and encourage him to stick on to his former role. That is when Sean spoke up and said the two sentences which were to change his life forever.

'Andrea, you are the one who convinced me to take on this new role. You are the one who insisted I learn about change management. I did not want this change. I was happy where I was. And now, when I have finally learnt how to accept that change, you are taking it away from me. Give me one chance. I will prove that your faith in me was never wrong,' Sean's voice was choking.

Andrea walked out of the room and called Dr Raheja, 'I want to reverse my decision. I am willing to take a chance and discount what Burjor said about Sean. I want to give Sean a chance. And if anything seems uncertain in times of need, I will don my surgical gloves again. The surgery department will not fail.'

'If that is what you think Andrea...that's fine,' said Dr Raheja at the other end.

January 2018.

Burjor's behaviour had changed dramatically. From being an ambitious, enthusiastic team member, he was now morose and rude. When she confronted him, she knew there was something wrong, something that was upsetting him and she needed to clear the air. What Andrea heard over the next three hours left her stunned. After much prodding, this is what Burjor said,

'The announcement of your arrival as the Head of Sunbeam is the worst thing that has ever hit me. I have worked in world-class hospitals in leadership positions. I joined Sunbeam with hope and gave it my best shot. Nobody can begin to imagine the kind of personal sacrifices I have made to get the surgeries in order and build the reputation that they command today. And suddenly they get someone else at the helm. I hate this designation. On top of which, you have created this caustic atmosphere. You and Parul are just two women fighting and innocent people have suffered. With the witch-hunt you have launched to get rid of all the people who used to report to Parul, you have ruined careers! When the first bits about you began to appear on social media, Parul wept. She felt so bad for you and you are alleging that she is responsible for instigating those comments!

You've been going around saying I don't do my work properly and that I don't take on smaller surgery projects at the cost of the big ones I do. Besides, people have had enough of your pep talk, your supposed inspirational stories and your unsolicited advice. Sending anyone to talk to you is a sure way of getting them to resign. I've cracked that joke myself about you. It is laughing stock.'

'That's not true Burjor. I was the one who sent out the email about your laudatory contribution. I told your team I trust you completely and that you will be running your surgery department till your last day at Sunbeam!' exclaimed Andrea.

Burjor gave her a wry smile, 'Too late and too little Andrea. Check your emails! Are you even aware of what you are doing? Maybe you need to meditate, do whatever! You didn't even copy me on that email to the team.'

Andrea was startled, 'Really I haven't? Dr Raheja even replied to everyone with his appreciation of your work. But Burjor I showed you what I had framed in that email on my laptop before sending it out. You do understand it is oversight that I have not copied you.'

'Oh, now you are going to hold this against me. It's not just about the email. You told me I should meet my targets before I leave...,' said Burjor.

'Of course, I did Burjor. I told you people leave organizations but the best way to leave is to outperform even during your notice period.

The entire Surgery department and so many others look up to you. I am sad that you are leaving. But as you have decided to move on, I would like to cite yours as an exemplary exit,' said Andrea.

'Oh yes, you threatened me that you would not give me a good reference if I don't meet my targets during the notice period! And now that I have said all this, you will ask me not to serve my notice period and leave tomorrow. That's what you've been doing with all those who used to report to Parul, set them up for failure and let them go, ruined careers,' smirked Burjor.

Shocked, Andrea took a step back.

'You know Burjor, first thing, thanks for saying all that you said. At least I know where you are coming from. Let me divide what you said into two parts:

Part 1: What is personal feedback for me, like me being watchful of my emails (taking a deep breath); I will accept, reflect and change. I cannot change anyone else but I can always change myself whenever the need arises. It has been a very stressful time with the resolving of the research department issues, Parul's direct reportees moving over to me and more. I have stretched myself beyond limits and the stress has showed. And the lies being perpetuated about me within the walls of this hospital and now on social media have not helped. I made a mistake, I reacted. That is not me and I need to go back to being me. So, I'm sorry about that.

Part 2: The rest of what you said about ruining careers and criticizing you is misrepresentation of facts and twisting of the truth. I will not accept that. Nobody has been asked to leave Sunbeam. They wanted to leave on their own and chose what they wanted to do with their lives and when. We have gone out of our way to support them with their personal situation whenever they have cited ill health, personal circumstances or anything else as the reason for wanting to leave. Each was given a choice of completing the assignment at hand or meeting a target and leaving at the end of their notice period. Some chose not to, and left earlier. If they have chosen to say one thing to some people and another outside, clearly instigated, it is part of the general misrepresentation that is prevalent here sadly.

About me saying anything wrong against you, that has never happened. I had a lot of hope from you when we started working again 10 months ago. I had a dream that each of you, especially you, would be at the head of a hospital unit that would be bigger than today's Sunbeam. Moreover, I believed that we shared a very positive work equation all these months. The most unfortunate aspect of this whole thing is that you, Burjor, believe every word of what you said.

'Of course, I do Andrea, why would I say anything if I do not believe it!' said Burjor.

'Anyway Burjor, the fabric of this equation, the milk is so spoilt that I simply have to pass by, I need not even say anything and I will be misunderstood, the milk will curdle anyway. I know for certain my conscience is clear. I have only wished the best for you and have gone out of my way to make sure you succeed at Sunbeam, Andrea walked away.'

The weeks passed with formal handover meetings between Burjor, his second in command, Rani and the new surgeon Sean. Being a brilliant organizer, Burjor's documentation was as precise as the scalpel he wielded in the operation theatre.

February 2018.

Burjor had refused a farewell. It was his last day of work. Andrea, Sean and Rani were busy with a Medical Council of India (MCI) visit. By the time Andrea reached her desk late in the afternoon, Burjor had left. His laptop, keys and gadgets lay on her desk with a note— 'Burjor's laptop and password'.

That evening, Rani came up to Andrea and resigned, citing personal reasons. In a meeting with Dr Raheja, Rani mentioned that one of her reasons for her resignation was that Andrea had sidelined her during the MCI visit.

When Andrea heard this, she sighed—the handover had taken three months to Rani who Burjor said knew everything there was to know and to Sean who Burjor said was a recipe for disaster being Andrea's blue-eyed boy. The saga which Andrea thought had just ended was to continue....

3 March 2018.

5 PM: Andrea, Sean and Nitin were engrossed in the numbers for next year, when Sean's beeper started ringing. Andrea's desk phone rang and so did her two mobile phones, all at the same time. The receptionist Melanie's panic-stricken voice on Andrea's desk phone uttered, 'There's been a road accident, a children's school bus has overturned and caught fire. The first two ambulances have arrived and others in cars/auto-rickshaws are on their way.'

Andrea sprang out of the room and Sean was already sprinting towards the operation theatre.

She briskly made her way to reception with crisp, curt instructions to the team,

'Nitin, could you call the police control room please and then ask your team to alert the Delhi blood bank and surgicals for additional oxygen as we need it? Also, could you ask Deepali and Joe from Admin to join Melanie at reception? She will need support.'

'Melanie, can you arrange for admission forms to be placed on the side tables please? Please open the ante room. People accompanying patients can sit there. If anyone from the police or media calls, please direct those calls to me. Please direct visitors from the media or police to the boardroom. I will see them there. We do not want to upset the parents and relatives of the injured any further.' And then to Col Jitendra Pal, Sunbeam's Head of Security, Andrea requested,

'Colonel, could we ensure strict adherence to process please? No one without a valid ID gets through the biometric barriers, no tail gaiting. No media, no police inside the surgical and treatment areas.'

For the next six hours, the team worked uninterrupted. It had been a 40-seater primary school bus and the crash had damaged the entire front half. The fire had been contained by the prompt action of well-wishers from the neighbourhood using their garden hosepipes. Most of the children seated at the back of the bus were just shocked by the jolt and were in the children's ward, being appeased by the nurses and some over-anxious ones, resting after very mild tranquilizers. Those seated in the middle of the bus had fractured limbs, some hairline cracks and others minor cuts and bruises. Sadia and team seemed to have these under control. In fact, Sadia had even left for the day as usual leaving the ward in the hands of her able and experienced nurses.

But Sean and Burjor's former team of surgeons were fighting the toughest battle. Though it was a children's hospital, two bystanders had rushed in the bus driver and bus conductor. Severely injured, with shards of glass sticking out and charred body parts, it had been a horrific sight. Unfortunately, neither had survived to tell the tale of what exactly led to this gruesome accident. Among the children, here were no casualties, just yet. A case of hip relocation had been operated successfully. Twin boys—one with a bruised wrist and another with a dislocated elbow—were now under observation but out of danger. But among those badly hurt were Siya (3) and her brother Aryan (9) who had been sitting just behind the driver. Aryan had suffered a deep gash on his forehead and chin, barely missing his right eye but cutting his lower lip. He was unable to bend his right knee. Sean had stitched up the gash under anaesthesia. The X-rays had not revealed any obvious internal injury. But the team knew that a seizure or convulsions at any point would be dangerous. Aryan was under observation in the ICU.

Strangely, Siya showed no apparent external injury. But as soon as she was admitted to the hospital, she vomited. And in the last six hours, even before she could be put through an X-ray to check internal injury and operate, her condition had deteriorated rapidly. An hour ago, she had suffered a severe cardiac arrest and was on an artificial heart–lung machine.

11 PM: While Sean battled to save the life of the siblings, Andrea and Nitin were in the boardroom dealing with a drama of a different kind—Siya and Aryan's devastated parents were outside the ICU, taking turns praying by their children's bedside. But in the boardroom the children's uncle had walked in—Jagan bhai from Ambala, a local politician with four lackeys and a police inspector in tow. They were demanding that Sunbeam produce the surgeon who had operated on Aryan before the police as it was obvious to them that there had been medical negligence in treating their niece and nephew. The uncle's explanation was that it was very suspicious to see that only Siya and Aryan were in Cardiac ICU while the other children were not. Even more suspicious to Jagan bhai was that Sunbeam had recently invested in importing a new heart and lung machine.

Even as Andrea and Nitin tried to reason with Jagan bhai saying that the surgeons needed to concentrate on the children's treatment at this point, the police inspector, straight out of a bad Bollywood flick, glared at Andrea, 'We'll see you at the Police station soon!'

Over the next 6 hours, Andrea walked the corridors of Sunbeam, requesting back-up surgical and nursing staff from a sister-hospital, asking Joe to organize cups of tea and food for the staff and the parents keeping vigil in the ante-room, interacting with the school authorities, battling the array of media questions.

Amid this, Andrea received intimation on four counts which she chose to keep aside for the time being.

Her priority was to ask for Siya's medical reports. In her 20-year career, she had not seen a case like this. Like Sean had expressed disbelief, she was baffled too. She had also called Dr Raheja to check if he had seen something akin to this during his longer career and he hadn't. She emailed those reports to three people she had looked up to and trusted during her career Alison George at the children's cardiac unit in London, Senthil at the paediatric specialty hospital in New York and Dr Joag at the paediatric wing of the medical college in Mumbai who had seen more ill children than Andrea could ever imagine. She marked all three emails 'Super urgent'.

She then turned to the disturbing intimations on four counts (all closer to her current location in Gurugram):

1. An online alert that someone had updated the social media site proclaiming that Andrea (apart from other things), had brought bad luck to Sunbeam Hospital and by some divine intervention, orchestrating an accident involving innocent children in its vicinity.

2. A leave application from Sadia specifying she will not be reachable during her time away, especially as she would not be paid during this period.

3. An email from Rani enlisting queries and complaints about Sean and his work style, when her last working day would be and seeking clarity on the company's policy on full and final settlement.

4. An alert from the communication team that Parul had been quoted in one of the online media channels talking about the accident and Sunbeam's efforts representing the company's management team.

Disturbed (more at her own idealism and left wanting to accept reality) that at least four or more individuals at Sunbeam who were clearly more interested in themselves than in saving children injured in the accident, or in Sunbeam's welfare, Andrea answered the two emails mechanically quoting hospital policy, but her heart and mind were with Siya, Aryan, their parents, Sean and his brave team of six battling with the children's lives.

4 AM: Among the many small changes that Andrea had been able to execute at Sunbeam, one was the establishment of a multi-faith prayer room in a quiet corner of the hospital. Andrea was not religious, she did not actually believe in idols or rituals, but she knew that a significant proportion of the Indian population did turn to scientifically unproven means when the doctors had finished trying and were waiting for outcome. The multi-faith prayer room was for the loved ones of the patients at Sunbeam.

At 4 AM, confident that the team that was helping save the critically ill children was as equipped and comfortable as they could be under the circumstances, Andrea found herself drawn to this prayer room. She knelt and for the first time in many hours felt the silence around her. She prayed for Aryan and Siya to get to their destiny in the shortest possible time with the least pain possible. Andrea's years in paediatrics had taught her that loved ones go through the turmoil of prolonging vegetative lives and bound by law and moral directives, paediatricians like her and Sean helped them extend the misery.

In the quiet darkness of the prayer room, Andrea's tears flowed—for the unenviable condition of the parents of those two children, the pain that the four emails had caused her amid this crisis, the pain that Parul, Sadia and most of all Burjor's absence of faith had caused her over the past few months and the number of times she had battled with her inner force that wanted her to step out of Sunbeam and Gurugram for good.

5 AM: Andrea walked up to the fourth floor to the cardiac ICU. Aryan and Siya's parents had sunk into the sofas in the anteroom, drained with exhaustion and uninterrupted tears. Sean had fallen asleep at his desk. Sadia's well trained nurses kept vigil as the machinery keeping little Siya alive whirred in the background.

Andrea walked up to Aryan's bed first. Sister Nirmala watching over him stood up and chirped, 'Not a single convulsion, no vomiting, no seizures Dr Andrea. Dr Sean just pronounced the boy out of danger! Praise the Lord Dr Andrea!'

Andrea thanked Sister Nirmala for her vigilance, patience and care and handed her ₹300 to offer at the altar. She knew Sister Nirmala was a devout church goer and would be lighting a candle and making an offering to her God for saving the child. As she walked back to her desk, she passed little Siya's bed. Sister Paula who was watching over Siya was diligently doing what Sadia had instructed her to do in her training manual. Every hour, check her vital signs and note them down in the record sheet, check if there was mucus up the child's throat and nose and remove it through the suction tube.

Through the process-driven actions around her, Siya appeared to be fast asleep, though with the lips turning blue at the edges and the swelling tongue starting to stick out.

6.30 AM: Aryan and Siya's parents, the Uncle Jagan bhai and Sean were seated in Andrea's room. She knew how badly they all needed coffees and teas and had arranged for some. Once they had downed the bittersweet potent liquids that got so much done against nature's forces of exhaustion, Andrea said,

'I feel truly blessed to tell you that your son Aryan is out of danger. In fact, we can move him out of the ICU today in a standard room and home in the next few days,' said Andrea. The parents couldn't stop crying, this time out of relief and folded their hands in gratitude and repeated over and over,

'Thank you, Dr Madam, God bless you!'

'If there is anyone who you may like to thank for this, it would be Dr Sean, his able team, Head Nurse Sadia and her able staff, especially Dr Nirmala,' said Andrea with a soft smile.

Sean smiled an exhausted smile.

After the couple thanked Sean and the God they worshipped, Andrea turned her computer screen to the three.

'Now let's talk about Siya's condition and the options we have,' began Andrea. She described how she had sent out three emails last night to different parts of the world, hoping for a miracle and a scientific explanation for what she was witnessing. The miracle was not to be but there was clarity and startling parity in what all three experts had said.

'Siya was suffering from a very rare genetic disorder. Her current condition in fact had nothing to do with the road accident. Yes, the vomiting could have been triggered by the jerks and shock of the collision but it could have easily been triggered by indigestion too. The verdict was that her condition was incurable and irreversible,' Andrea candidly showed them the emails and the scientific journals they had quoted.

The father broke down, the mother looked stunned, even apologetic— was her own genetic makeup responsible for her child's condition?

Jagan bhai stood up, 'I'll call the media. We were the landlords, the kings of our region. Nothing is wrong with our generation. How dare you talk about our lineage!! It is you Western influenced people who are creating these stories now that your Sean has made a mistake!' he shouted.

This time round, Siya and Aryan's father raised his palm requesting silence.

'*Chhote, chup kar* (Keep quiet junior). Dr Andrea, Dr Sean, what do you suggest we do? Any surgery, we are ready to spend anything, don't even think of the expenses.'

Andrea looked at Sean and delivered the painful verdict,

'Sir the only option is to switch off the machines. Your daughter cannot recover from this condition. Right now, only the machines are keeping her breathing and her heart beating.'

Both parents broke down and in stark contrast to cultural norms he was used to, the husband put his arm around his wife's shaking shoulders. Jagan, angry, sad, helpless against the powers far beyond his own, banged his fist on Andrea's glass office table in frustration.

March 10.

2 PM: The formalities were over. Siya's parents had quietly signed the documents put before them. Their baby's corneas were to go to a six-year-old boy in another part of the State waiting for a donor. They had also offered the child's body for post mortem so that the doctors could understand the condition better as well as for further medical research.

Sean, Andrea and Sadia (along with a weeping Sister Paula) stood next to little Siya's bed as the machinery was switched off. The tears of the parents refused to stop knowing that in the next hour or two, their beloved daughter would be no more. Jagan stood in a corner angry with the world. In the neighbouring room, the corneas were being prepared for transplant and downstairs, Sister Nirmala held Aryan in a tight embrace telling him how much she would miss him now that he was going home....

6 PM: Andrea and Sean sat in her room sharing the work chemistry over a cup of coffee that only love at the workplace can instil and courage demonstrated at the workplace can consolidate.

'So proud of you Sean! Keep up the good work. The surgery department is in good hands again. If anything, you are a recipe for success and once again, I'm sorry for believing the nonsense about the recipe for disaster,' said Andrea.

'Andrea, I saw you shed the tears for Siya's departure from a vegetative life and saw your joy at Aryan's departure to the life ahead of him! You will win some of us and you will lose some of us. Be prepared to show the courage you always do...,' smiled Sean.

## Analysing Courage at the Workplace

### The Solution Matrix—3-DEM Applied to Courage

As we established, the answer to managing emotion lies in the confluence of the following three: (a) the arts (b) management science (c) medical science.

*Building the 3-DEM Action Plan: Leveraging Courage at the Workplace*

Table 5.1 shows the stages of events at work that demonstrate courage to overcome obstacles. With the wealth of inspirational stories and examples of courage available in generic literature and history, each of these stages have been ably supported by a famous quote.

**Table 5.1** Stages of Demonstrating Courage at the Workplace

| Stage 1 | Stage 2 | Stage 3 | Stage 4 | Stage 5 | Stage 6 | Stage 7 |
|---------|---------|---------|---------|---------|---------|---------|
| Shock of problem | Crisis boiling over | Fight/Flight response | Emergency response | Persistent crisis | Success/ Failure | Fallouts of courage |
| Fear, insecurity, loneliness, anger, | Struggle against the problem, dejection, helplessness | Acceptance, question care/ commitment towards outcome | Taking charge, being in the moment | Failure, try again, resilience, courage osmosis | Delight on success, relief on ease of pressure | Emotional exhaustion |

*Source:* Authors.

As we can see, acceptance (Stage 3) is the turning point. Once the crisis is acknowledged and accepted, the response changes from defensive to proactive.

**Stage 1**

> *Bran thought about it. 'Can a man still be brave if he's afraid?' 'That is the only time a man can be brave,' his father told him.*
>
> — George R. R. Martin, *A Game of Thrones*

In Stage 1, we learn that the demonstration of courage needs a negative situation to begin with.

**Stage 2**

> *This world demands the qualities of youth; not a time of life but a state of mind, a temper of the will, a quality of the imagination, a predominance of courage over timidity, of the appetite for adventure over the life of ease.*
>
> — Robert F. Kennedy

Stage 2 shows us that true courage is demonstrated during a sustained period of crisis or when a person is stretched beyond his/her comfort zone. It also tells us that people who demonstrate courage refuse to accept the status quo when they see and acknowledge that something is not going right.

**Stage 3**

> *From caring comes courage.*
>
> —Lao Tzu

Stage 3 is critical because it pushes us to question whether the cause we are fighting for is worth the effort, time, money and sacrifice. If we conclude that it is not worth the sacrifice, we give up, we take flight. When we accept that the vision/goal of what we would accomplish is worth the fight, we stay on. We stay on and fight because we care.

## Stage 4

Lao Tzu's words of wisdom point towards the core of courage. The individual demonstrating courage needs to bear the 'cost of leadership' in terms of time, effort, often health and other personal possessions. Tzu's words also indicate that courage summons the person to get up and act and not wait for something to happen to her/him.

> *Have the courage to follow your heart and intuition.*
> *They somehow already know what you truly want to*
> *become. Everything else is secondary.*
>
> —Steve Jobs, Stanford commencement
> speech, June 2005

Courage is mustered not only when the individual lives in the moment but also when the individual is able to visualize a future of success and lives the moments of courage as if they were transient in the journey towards the creation of the miracle.

## Stage 5

> *Courage doesn't always roar. Sometimes courage*
> *is the little voice at the end of the day that says*
> *I'll try again tomorrow.*
>
> —Mary Anne Radmacher

*Success is not final. Failure is not fatal.*
*It is the courage to continue that counts.*

—Winston Churchill

Courage as we said, is the response generated by a crisis, a need. But even when courage is generated and begins to act, the biggest test is the patience and resilience needed to continue when there appears to be no end in sight.

Leaders have infused courage among teams and populations inspiring mutinies, revolution, movements leading to individuals willing to even sacrifice their lives for a cause.

## Stage 6

*You gain strength, courage, and confidence by every*
*experience in which you really stop to look fear in the*
*face. You are able to say to yourself, 'I lived through this*
*horror. I can take the next thing that comes along'.*

— Eleanor Roosevelt

When you can visualize a future that has overcome the situation that you are enduring today, this 'moment of living in retrospect' offers you the strength to continue and spur courage among the people you lead; this is called courage osmosis.

Leaders have built nations on courage osmosis—leveraging on the love people had for their cause and ultimately also for their leaders.

But the demonstration of courage has its share of negative impact—the damage caused to relationships at the workplace and to people who may not be as committed to the cause at hand or as courageous (Figure 5.1).

**Figure 5.1**   Courage and Collateral Damage

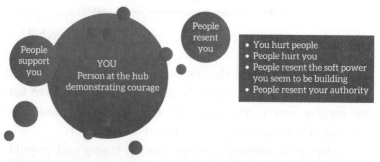

People support you

YOU
Person at the hub
demonstrating courage

People resent you

- You hurt people
- People hurt you
- People resent the soft power you seem to be building
- People resent your authority

- People align with your vision
- People go beyond the call of duty to support this vision
- People start demonstrating extreme courage themselves to overcome the crisis
- Courage osmosis continues further down the chain

*Source:* Authors.

The fence sitters are afraid to align. They will wait to see which way the wind will blow and then decide to support, to demonstrate courage and whether to act in the interest of the organization. Till the lines of power are unclear, they will do the minimum possible to survive, essentially duck under covers of inaction.

In Andrea's case, as per the *Navrasa* theory, the state of the *rasa* manifests due to the cause or trigger of the emotion (*vibhav*), the effect of the emotion is the *anubhava* and the transient/related emotions are the *vyabhichari*. While *rasas* denote the mood, these *bhavas* (associated with each *rasa*) create the mood through physical media—the brain, body or action.

Table 5.2, based on the arts, helps us classify the emotions connected with the dominant emotion of courage.

**Table 5.2**  Emotions Connected with the Dominant Mood of Courage

| Vibhav (Cause) | Sthahi Bhav (Dominant Emotion) | Anubhava (Experience) | Vyabhichari (Related Emotions) | Response | | |
|---|---|---|---|---|---|---|
| | Veer Rasa | | | Uttama (High) | Madhyama (Medium) | Adhama (Low) |
| Negative actions/ events leading to positive emotion | Courage | Stress, insult, hurt, fear, anger, helplessness | Fighter spirit<br><br>Pushing the boundaries | Assertive words, actions. Not reacting even in the face of extreme provocation | Stress, anger at the cause of the situation that has resulted in the need to display courage | Tantrum throwing |

## How can you apply the 5A framework?

How could Andrea have dealt with the burning need to demonstrate courage? The answer is by applying the 5As framework.

| 1 | Acknowledge | This situation needs me to take a decision. If I want to achieve the dream I came to build, I must stay on and not walk away from the situation. | I need to demonstrate courage. The kind of courage that is needed to combat these forces is different from the kind of situations I have faced before. |
|---|---|---|---|
| 2 | Analyse | It will help to put into categories what I'm really feeling (refer to nine emotions discussed) and understand at least some of what happens in the brain. | I feel sorrow at being victimized. I feel angry that I was stupid enough to go out of my way for people who have now let me down. I feel disgust that people lie through their teeth and have got away with it. I am fearful that my actions will continue to be misconstrued. |
| 3 | Accept | Courage is preceded by pain. If you have an ecosystem where you want to achieve what seemed impossible at your workplace, some would want to fall in place, others may want to rebel, still others would blame you for their failure to perform. | I have allowed my co-workers to touch my core. If they do not behave in the way I expect them to, it affects me much more than it would if they were just co-workers. |

*(continued)*

(continued)

| 4 | Administer | I will 'choose' my attitude. | I need to create an environment where people are forced to choose whether they want to be with me on this path of courage or be held back by inertia, disloyalty or fear. |
|---|---|---|---|
| 5 | Act | I will 'follow' my plan. | At this moment, it is time to focus and act. Men and women need to be inspired to demonstrate courage and follow through with action plans. Those who do not want to follow plans, need to be placed in an environment where they at least do not hamper execution of plans. |

# References

Crenshaw, Theresa L. 1997. *The Alchemy of Love and Lust*. New York: Putnam.

Dabbs, James McBride, and Mary Godwin Dabbs. 2000. *Heroes, Rogues, and Lovers: Testosterone and Behavior*. New York City, NY: McGraw-Hill.

Henderson, J. 2005. *A Life of Ernest Starling*. 1st Edition. London: Academic Press.

Tardanico, Susan. 2013. '10 Traits of Courageous Leaders.' Available at: https://www.forbes.com/sites/susantardanico/2013/01/15/10-traits-of-courageous-leaders/#11626d334fc0

# Anger

*Anybody can become angry—that is easy; but to be angry with the right person and to the right degree and at the right time and for the right purpose, and in the right way—that is not within everybody's power and is not easy.*

—Aristotle

# Background/Overview

Here is an old but apt little joke:

A lady was buying groceries as her toddler was throwing tantrums. The mum and daughter were waiting in a queue to pay for the groceries, and the daughter continued to wail demanding that the Mum to buy a toy as well. The Mum continued to push her shopping cart patiently. Though she looked angry, she repeated in a mild tone,

'Calm down Jessica; it's okay Jessica; we are going home really quick.' A shopper walked up to the lady and said,

'I really admire your patience. The way you have been telling your daughter Jessica to calm down and that it is all okay!' The lady shot him a glance, her frustration brimming over and replied,

'No.... My name is Jessica!'

As per our survey, of all people who left jobs due to emotional issues,

- 43 per cent left because anger was the emotion that made them quit.
- 30 per cent also admit that they have leveraged anger to increase productivity.

# Depicting Anger in the Arts

Anger in the traditional performing arts usually shows imagery of a form with the body erect, often wielding a weapon, the eyes blazing, the determined chin, poised to attack the victim that more often than not denotes the evil. The imagery assumes grotesque forms to highlight the impact of the wrath that is generated to 'eradicate human suffering and evil' including the tongue sticking out, a goddess astride a tiger, a God donning snakes around his neck and more.

In its subtler forms, the anger of the heroines in the performing arts could be directed at more personalized situations like irritation at a factor that keeps her away from a loved one or sulking at a loved one for being away!

*Anger is the prelude to courage.*

—Eric Hoffer

Hebb (1946) called humans 'the most emotional of animals'. People get angry all the time; sometimes it goes unnoticed. Getting angry with their smartphones freezing or computers going slow and road rage are all around us. How you want the person at the receiving end to feel is up to you.

If it weren't for the law, some business users would be up for a fist fight with the IT team. IT will hit back equally. A workplace can ignore laughter and all other emotions, but expressions of anger are always under the scanner—people swearing at their computers and punching their keyboards—sometimes making headlines for the wrong reasons. Everyone has a choice to either get a constructive or a destructive outcome from this amazing emotion called anger. Anger at the workplace has resulted in so many revolutionary changes. Gender equality at work, equal pay, minimum wage, laws that protect rights of workers were because people had felt a certain degree of anger and wanted to do something about these things and positively used the emotion to bring about the change.

Anger can sometimes 'possess' a person, and when it's a senior who becomes angry, it can lead to the whole business being brought to its knees. Similarly, if there are people or a person who is angry and it is at the lower level in management, this could be a source to know something that no one knows. A source of feedback that does not show up on the employee survey form.

Anger is simple yet complex which is why it is felt by every human being differently. And it is okay to get angry. Let me repeat this:

'It is okay to get angry.'

Getting angry is normal, but the way you respond is where the trick lies. If used in the right way, it can do wonders, if not, it can be disastrous. The response of anger ranges from small frustration to huge breakouts that result in feisty fights, impacting the body and mind.

## The Science Behind Anger

So, what happens to us when we are angry? Our heart rate, arterial tension and testosterone production increases, cortisol (the stress hormone) decreases, and the left hemisphere of the brain becomes more stimulated.[1]

Normally, when we get angry we show a natural tendency to get closer to what made us angry to try to eliminate it.

Therefore, anger or provocation inspires or pushes us to act.

Anger is the normally expected response by the brain to any threats it can foresee. The body releases adrenaline, the muscles tighten, the heart rate and blood pressure increases and a red flushed look may show up on the face.

---

[1] https://dailyhealthpost.com/anger-negatively-affects-brain-and-heart/

Amygdala is the part of the brain that picks up the emotion of anger. It is located in the temporal lobe of the brain.

Amygdala manages the emotional instinct of 'fight or flight' when fear is felt and when feeling threatened and stressed (Hebb 1946). It is a system designed to react first and then analyse.

Just above the amygdala inside the frontal lobe is the ability to make decisions, solve problems and control behaviour.[2] When you feel anger, blood gushes into the frontal cortex underpinning rational thought, and that is when there is an instinctive reaction which could be good or bad (Herrero et al. 2010). It is to avoid that instinctive, instant reaction why it is recommended that you should count from 1 to 10 when you feel angry.

If you find someone who is an 'angeraholic', it is the because of the frequent anger damaging the brain. A continued supply of small shots of anger bursts would mean that the brain will ultimately lose the ability to control anger in any form.

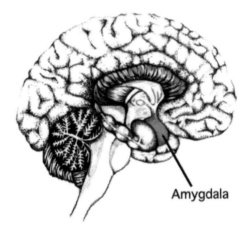

Amygdala

---

[2] https://www.sciencedaily.com/releases/2010/05/100531082603.htm

Here is the strange part, if we all know so much about managing anger then why is it that we still get angry? Being angry is an emotion that is very normal in human beings. It is one of the most basic primitive emotions. It's a part of our brain's operating system. Though negative, most of the times it is a way to express and communicate.

Anger has got nothing to do with what is happening around you in your workplace. It is all about what is happening inside your own brain when you are experiencing that outside world.

Anger for the cave man was a very useful tool. It was used to compete for food and survival. The brain is set up to identify anger in other human beings; even an infant can tell the difference between a happy and an angry face. This can then be used for or in a situation to get the desired result.

# Dashrath's story

This is a story of a man who got so angry with a mountain that he moved it. Dashrath Manjhi ran away from his home at a young age and worked at Dhanbad's coal mines in India. He returned to his village and married Falguni Devi. While crossing Gehlour hills to bring him lunch, Falguni slipped and injured herself seriously, which eventually led to her death. Manjhi was deeply angry and disturbed and that very night decided to carve a path through the Gehlour hills so that his village could have easier access to medical attention. He carved a path 110 m long, 7.7 m deep in places and 9.1 m wide to form a road through the rocks in Gehlour hill. He said,

'When I started hammering the hill, people called me a lunatic, but that steeled my resolve.'

He completed the work in 22 years (1960–82). This path reduced the distance between the Atri and Wazirganj sectors of the Gaya district from 55 km to 15 km. Though mocked for his efforts, he has made life easier for people of Gehlour village. Later, Manjhi said, 'Though most villagers taunted me at first, there were quite a few who lent me support later by giving me food and helping me buy my tools.'

Dashrath chose to use the anger he was feeling in a positive way and moved a mountain.

What mountain can you move with your anger?
    Following is an excerpt from a news article on anger and how it can at times have an unlikely impact.

# Juli's story

50-year-old Juli Briskman showed the finger to US President Donald Trump's motorcade in November 2017 and was fired by her employer after a photo of the incident went viral.

And what reason was given by her employer—government contractor Akima LLC? Not that she had flipped the bird at the president, but that she violated the firm's social media policy by using the photo as her profile picture on Facebook and Twitter.

The image of Briskman on a bicycle, giving the middle finger to Trump's motorcade as the vehicles made their way along a road in Sterling, Virginia, was taken by a White House photographer travelling with the President.

At the time, Trump was going back from his golf course to the White House. Briskman was out for a Saturday bike ride when the convoy of black SUVs drove past.

The photo went viral soon after and was used by numerous media outlets around the world. The next day, her bosses called her for a meeting and informed her that she had violated the firm's social media policy by using the photo as her profile picture.

The bosses also told her that the photo could hurt Akima's business as a government contractor.

Briskman, who was part of Akima's marketing team for more than six months, said she explained that she wasn't at work when the incident happened, and her social media pages did not name her employer.

She also explained what was going through her head when she gave the middle finger to Trump's motorcade several times on that day.

'My finger said what I was feeling. I'm angry, and I'm frustrated,' she told CNN.

Briskman listed the reasons for her anger at Trump. 'Healthcare doesn't pass, but you try to dismantle it from the inside,' she said. 'Five hundred people get shot in Las Vegas; you're doing nothing about it. You know, white supremacists have this big march and hurt a bunch of people down in Charlottesville, and you call them good people.'

She added that she was also angry because Trump was on the golf course at a time when the US administration was dealing with several major problems, such as the damage caused by two hurricanes in Puerto Rico.

Anger got the better of her, anyway. Briskman got angry, and unfortunately, the only person who was impacted from her actions was herself.

## The Solution Matrix

Look at the following table, then try and identify the patterns you feel when you get angry. It explains why anger is triggered and what you experience.

| Vibhav (Cause) | Sthahi Bhav (Dominant Emotion) | Anubhava (Experience) | Vyabhichari (Related Emotions) | Long-term Impact |
|---|---|---|---|---|
| Frustration, inability to change the situation | Anger | Less caution, less reasoning, urge to dominate, impulsive, heightened expression, fast heartbeats, blood pressure increase, muscles tense up sweaty, flushed body | Guilt, hurt, fear, insult | Poor immune system, heart attack, stroke, headache, higher blood pressure, respiratory disorders, skin disorders, circulatory disorders |

## Applying the 5A framework:

| 1 | Acknowledge | Acknowledging anger is easy. Sometimes people around you acknowledge your anger even before you do. Most of the times you will have the same patterns. Patterns you once identify you can make a note of and then acknowledge for future. When you find yourself in a difficult situation, what really happens? The question is not what you are doing about the anger; it is what is anger doing to you? Do you start feeling stress around your neck, do you tighten your fist or tap your feet quickly? Look out for the common physical triggers that you experience when you think you were angry on previous occasions. And acknowledge. And tell yourself, 'There is anger building up in me.' |
|---|---|---|
| 2 | Analyse | There is a list of questions further down the chapter that will help you analyse why you are angry. A way to do it is to write down all the elements or ecosystem around you. Maybe make a list of the elements you came across in the last few hours. Family, traffic, the person at the coffee shop, office reception, line manager, sitting in a hot meeting room, an email you read you did not like. And then point out to the element that might have triggered the process of anger. |
| 3 | Accept | Accepting anger is no doubt difficult. Once you know you are angry, focus on accepting it. It is that thin line between knowing you are angry and doing something about it. The space in between—that space could be few seconds. But just isolate your mind for a moment and self-talk and accept—'Yes, I am aware I am angry.' For example, taking deep breaths is not accepting anger, you are already trying to remedy it. It is that moment when you accept that you are angry and then decide that you should take deep breaths to manage your anger. |

| 4 | Administer | Figuring out what to do about the anger you are now aware of and accepting that you feel it requires practice. There is always time to respond. The general rule is don't do anything at the spur of the moment. If you do want to or are getting any ideas, hold them off for a moment. Do you get angry while you attend a meeting and listen to someone who tells you it's rubbish? Wait for the meeting with an action in mind that you will do once the meeting is over. Before you do think of any action, I would strongly suggest you go through the questions mentioned further down in the chapter and decide the best course of action. These are powerful questions that help break the anger pattern and think logically. |
|---|---|---|
| 5 | Act | Taking action to manage anger could be easy or difficult. Often when it relates to anger, then doing could be well within or way outside the comfort zone. If you are angry with someone in the workplace, taking some deep breaths is an easy action in which you have used a typical trick to kill anger. But if the action is to have a tough conversation with someone, it could be outside the comfort zone. Whenever you try something to manage your anger, make a note and review what worked in your mind several times. It will help you set and select the best course of action for future. |

# Tools/Tips/Worksheets

## How Angry Are You?

Following is a thermometer you can use. Take it as a scale to measure anger or, in fact, any feeling.

Let's play! Think of the last time you were angry and put it in the scale. In fact, as you run through the whole journey measure every moment and where it stood on the scale that follows.

Something to note when facing anger is that 'easy' will mean different things to different people based on the experience they have had in their lives.

An example is a meeting where a team is told they will be made redundant. John may end up selecting 'still quite easy' as he has been through redundancy before. And Simon may select 'can't handle it' as he has not experienced one before. In the same case, John could also select 'out of control' although he has experienced it a number of times before, but this time he is in huge debts, which now means John is in big trouble.

Thermometer:

1. Easy
2. Still quite easy
3. Just a little uneasy
4. Starting to bother
5. Not too good
6. Getting tough
7. Pretty tough
8. Really tough
9. Can't handle it
10. Out of control

A professor used to share this story at the beginning of every year about how perception changes the mood. Here it is:

## The story of perception

A father was travelling on the train with his 2 sons who were 4 and 6 years old. They sat in the coach that was meant to be 'quiet zone'. As the father stared out of the window, the two children were being a little more than naughty and making a lot of noise. There was an old lady who was trying to read the newspaper and was angry as she could not focus on her reading. There was another man who was staring at his phone screen, possibly reading something and was getting distracted and wasn't happy either.

Another lady trying to catch some sleep looked annoyed too. The other commuters on the train were not happy with the commotion the kids were making. All had a different level of anger building in them. Finally, one commuter stood up and walked to the father. He said in a displeased voice,

'Would you mind telling your kids to be a little quiet? You do realize you have boarded the quiet coach?' The father startled, looked at the gentleman and across the coach and at the annoyed and angry faces. He said 'We are just heading home from their mother's funeral who passed away last week. They don't understand what has happened and that their mother who is my wife will never be back again. I don't know how to explain this to them and don't want to stop them from being happy as it'll be a matter of few hours or days before they truly understand what has happened!' The whole coach went quieter than it was before. Everyone was angry at different levels, but now everyone felt sad and guilty. Soon, they were responding to the smiles of the boys.

Perception is very powerful. Sometimes changing the perspective can cure the angriest of situations. There is no single best tip that works to control anger. Every human is unique and every human will have their own way to manage anger. Following are some techniques you can use to manage anger:

1.  *Five-second rule:* It is very easy to get driven by anger and say things that one will regret later. Have you heard a couple fight where one of the partners ended up saying something one knew he/she should not have said, but said it anyway? The 'bring it on' attitude does not go well with managing anger.

    Count backwards before you say something—5, 4, 3, 2, 1. It's like giving a 5-second break to allow some breathing space before you say what you want to.

It gives time to reconsider the words and focus on the right phrase.

2.  *Stop, watch, go:* To manage anger, think traffic lights. There is a need to be careful not to express anger based on instinct, but it is equally important to let it out at some point. Once you have held back and are now ready to give a calculated reply without expressing anger, challenge yourself and sprinkle a bit of anger in it. Don't put others outside their comfort zone but express that you felt the same.

3.  *Walk, run, breathe:* Diversion for the brain can work wonders. When you get angry, there is an emotion that is on a high. Want to diffuse, push your body outside the comfort zone by doing some physical activity. Physical activity can help reduce the stress that causes you to become angry. If you feel your anger escalating, go for a brisk walk or run, or spend some time doing other enjoyable physical activities.

4.  *A quickie break:* Parents often give their kids timeout when they are misbehaving. A mini-break before carrying on a task or a conversation for kids that they are getting impatient about. The same rule and technique can work on adults—taking what I call 'quickie break' or a timeout or going out for a walk. Have you ever seen people walk out of meetings to take a cigarette break? That should not be the only reason to step out. Breathing in some oxygen will fuel up your brain with the right emotions.

5.  *Breathe slowly:* Inhale and exhale in longer breaths than you normally do. When angry, your body wants to breathe in and out quicker and doing the opposite

helps calm the anger the down. It puts the brain on an emergency brake from the anger pattern it is in, allowing you to stop and think.

6. *What would your superhero do:* When you know you are getting angry, think of your favourite superhero. It could be Wonder Woman or Superman or a manager you know. What would their response be like? And then think how they would respond if they were in the same situation.

7. *Switch off from anger at work:* This is one I struggled with personally for a long time. There should be a routine to get into work mode by dressing up formally. There should also be a routine to get into the home mode by dressing casually and making a list of things to do to feel at home. It could be having a shower, or may be just enjoying a glass of wine—your personal list to welcoming yourself back at home every day.

8. *Listen to music:* Remember the 3-DEM model. Use music to manage anger. Listen to a song with high beats per minute; it will help you diffuse and vent out the anger you have and listening to a slow number could help you transform the energy while angry and slow it down. The cricketing hero Sachin Tendulkar in his movie 'Sachin' has mentioned that he had a habit of listening to the same song repeatedly to calm his nerves. If this can work for Mr Cool, then why not for us? Select a random song, a song that would trigger the emotional state you want to be in and listen to it again and again and again. The same song. Your mind will eventually transit into the state you are looking for. Music is magic.

# Let's Play

Below is a checklist to find out what often triggers anger in you. Rate these on a scale of 1–10. 1 being easy and 10 being out of control.

| | Easy–Out of control | | | | | | | | | |
|---|---|---|---|---|---|---|---|---|---|---|
| | 1 | 2 | 3 | 4 | 5 | 6 | 7 | 8 | 9 | 10 |
| Being ignored by someone | | | | | | | | | | |
| Being made to wait | | | | | | | | | | |
| Being kept hungry due to a meeting | | | | | | | | | | |
| Being cheated in office politics | | | | | | | | | | |
| Being misunderstood | | | | | | | | | | |
| Being made a part of rumour or gossip | | | | | | | | | | |
| Being hurt | | | | | | | | | | |
| Being given bad news like no salary increment | | | | | | | | | | |
| Being given unfair treatment | | | | | | | | | | |
| Feeling stressed | | | | | | | | | | |
| Being criticized | | | | | | | | | | |
| Feeling tired in office | | | | | | | | | | |
| Being disrespected | | | | | | | | | | |
| Noise workplace | | | | | | | | | | |
| Being left out in the team | | | | | | | | | | |
| Being interrupted | | | | | | | | | | |
| Being told what to do | | | | | | | | | | |
| Not knowing what to do | | | | | | | | | | |

Use the following chart to rate yourself. Play from the heart and don't try and get a high score. Rate the numbers that you 'feel' are closest.

| A (score 10) | B (score 8) | C (score 6) | D (score 2) | Your score |
|---|---|---|---|---|
| I am calm and happy | I am not that happy | I am always irritated | I am always angry | |
| I sometimes feel frustrated | I feel irritated | I have voices arguing in my head | I always look for negative in others | |
| I do get angry but occasionally | I keep things to myself | I feel like a victim | I get angry beyond limits | |
| I am very expressive | I avoid conflicts | I can lash out anytime | I am dangerous when I am angry | |

Depending on your score, see the table below that explains the score.

A:    10—Less angry
B:    8—Angrier
C:    6—Seriously angry
D:    10—Dangerous angry

An ideal score will be 10; if you are any less:

Think of a situation from the past which makes you justify that score and then use the following section to see how you would have dealt with it in a different way.

Play around with this template as much as you can in real life scenarios you have experienced. You will get to tame your anger better.

# Question Quotient

During a coaching session, people often share moments of anger from or with someone; there are these powerful questions to help them reflect and look at things from a different perspective. My suggestion is to bookmark this page, and whenever you feel angry, go through the list and try and answer as many as questions as you can.

1. How do you manage to get angry?

   Reflect on the situation you are going through, and how you managed to get yourself from the previous emotional state you were in to anger. You could have been happy, and then something triggered the anger. Maybe you were stressed and came to know that something bad was about to happen, and the moment you saw it coming, you became angry and put your defences up.

2. Who says it is not okay to get angry?

   We are often told it is not okay to be angry and that anger invites trouble. I would invite you to challenge your thinking, and once you know you have been angry about something, challenge yourself. If you are feeling guilty about being angry, who says it is not right to be angry? What you do with that anger is altogether a different question. But to feel anger is okay; it's all part of being a human being.

3. What would you do instead if you were not angry?

   Come up with a Plan B. If you do not want to be angry or were told to choose some other emotion, what would it be? Will you choose to be angrier or calm?

4. Do you get angry with that person and when?

   Anger is inside of the person who is feeling it. Anger is more about the situation than the person. And a way to remember that is to think that if you were to meet this person, whom you are feeling the anger towards now, at a Pub or Christmas party or any social gathering, would you still be angry. Visualising this often helps separate the person you are angry with from the emotion of anger itself.

5. If you had to teach me how to get angry, how would it be?
   Give yourself an expert lesson on the process to get angry. What is step 1? What needs to trigger it? Which part of the body feels it first? What happens next?

6. How would you know if that wasn't true?
   Sometimes even knowing that you shouldn't be angry with the person, you still are. Here is a question to answer. How do you know that the reason behind your anger is true and what if it wasn't? If it is, what evidence do you have to be sure it is true?

7. What would happen if you did not get angry?
   Sometimes letting go is the best cure or knowing it is okay to feel angry. Knowing you are angry and feeling guilty or feeling okay about it can make a huge difference in the way it is dealt with.

8. What would happen if you showed your anger?
   What is the worst-case scenario? Leaning into your fear and going outside your comfort zone is not always a bad thing. It is okay to show or register your anger without harming anyone.

9. How would you like to respond with that anger?
   Responding to the person you are angry with or the situation you are angry at and responding to the anger itself are two different perspectives. Ever dealt with an angry person where you choose to let the person cool

down before you talk about what happened? When you are the one who is angry, always think about responding to your own anger first before reflecting on who or what triggered it.

10. How will getting angry affect the wider systems around you?

In that moment of anger, it is very natural to forget about the wider systems. The story about Briskman showing the finger to the president's car ended up costing her job. There is a wider system around us—workplace, customers, stakeholders, home, family, bills, kids, health. Getting angry sometimes can have a massive impact on any of those—sometimes in a way we never imagined. It is always good to assess the wider systems around you that will be impacted by the anger you are about to express.

11. How specifically angry are you?

Can you tell me, how specifically are you angry? Be as specific as you can. A simple way to control or assess anger is to ask yourself how specifically am I angry—less, more, more than average. The impact is not in the answer you give; the impact lies in the process trying to look for an answer. Use the thermometer recommended earlier.

12. What specifically is making you angry?

What is the exact issue that is making you angry? Pinpoint it. Is it the way your colleague said something, or was it what was said, or was it the choice of words used to say that message, or the location, or the timing of the event? Think like a surgeon and identify the nerve that is causing you anger.

13. How will you feel when that is not an issue anymore? Anger is an outcome of being overstressed or at times holding up something inside your own mind. Ask yourself which is the main issue that triggered the anger and what if that wasn't an issue anymore. Will you still be angry? If not angry, how will you feel instead?

Anger is a very strong emotion at work. If 43 per cent of people left their jobs because of anger, then anger needs to be accepted and managed. Challenge yourself to think and lean into this fear of feeling okay about being angry, not reflecting it as anger at the same time. Select carefully what you would like to do—destroy a relationship or career or dissolve the issue. If you haven't done it, go back to the 'let's play' section and do a health check. Is your anger healthy?

# References

Hebb, D. O. 1946. 'Emotion in Man and Animal: An Analysis of the Intuitive Processes of Recognition.' *Psychological Review* 53(2): 88–106. Available at https://philpapers.org/rec/HEBEIM (accessed on 25 June 2018).

Herrero, Neus, Marien Gadea, Gabriel Rodríguez-Alarcón, Raúl Espert, and Alicia Salvador. 2010. 'What Happens When We Get Angry? Hormonal, Cardiovascular and Asymmetrical Brain Responses.' *Hormones and Behavior* 57(3): 276. doi: 10.1016/j.yhbeh.2009.12.008.

# Laughter

*There are some things so serious you have to laugh at them.*

—Niels Bohr

# Background/Overview

- Over 63 per cent of the people surveyed have successfully used or leveraged laughter to improve the pace or quality of their work.
- Over 77 per cent survey respondents feel that their workplace would benefit from new or improved support and resources for dealing with strong emotions while at work.

## Laughter in the Arts

The performing arts beautifully make a fine distinction between smile, giggle and gregarious laughter. The finesse described in *The Natyashastra* accords the 'level' of each person in the social order and the maintenance of propriety in demonstrating emotion. This is especially distinct of *hasya* (laughter/humour/mirth). Across cultures, the depiction of laughter in the arts would show an individual with abroad smile, displaying teeth and twinkling eyes. A protagonist of a 'higher order' expected to exercise restraint in displaying all emotions would not guffaw or backslap. Moreover, they may not find slapstick humour funny at all and would seek situational comedy or satire for true entertainment. But whether it is in Western or Eastern cultures, the court jester or the essential comic as an integral part of theatre would wear clothes that would elicit laughter and use make-up and body language that would at least elicit a smile in the most restrained of individuals.

Even in the modern context, some cultures naturally smile and laugh more than others.

## The Science of Laughter

The 'happiness chemicals' or DOSE (dopamine, oxytocin, serotonin and endorphin) are triggered because of humour.

Laughter or humour is a very effective emotion to help take away negative emotions such as anger and frustration. Laughter alone can distract a person's mood away from the conformity of daily routines and stress of daily tasks we all experience.

Leaders and managers understand that these daily stresses can have a huge impact on productivity and quality of the work being done, but the knowledge is often brushed aside using the statement 'Keep emotions outside workplace'. Humour is the easiest and most cost-effective way to make an employee or oneself experience a positive rather than a negative emotion. It is one of the most advanced emotional intelligence (EI skills) in Mayer and Salovey's view. This is especially seen in a workplace, where complaining and a negative emotion can reduce and kill productivity (McGhee 2012).

A manager who wants to leverage using emotions can use humour through innovative approaches to introduce fun at work and keep negative emotions away.

Laugher is one emotion where the impact will multiply when emoted at the team level. If we were to compare the team to a basket of fruits, all fruits should be kept fresh to avoid any rotting. The team needs to be laughing together at themselves or something else to really leverage the emotion. When teams start feeling safe to laugh around with other teammates and anyone in the business, it is bound to have a positive impact on productivity and quality.

## Humour at the workplace—the pandas

If it wasn't for the fun we were having at work, the attrition rate would have been so much higher and the team spirit would not have had existed!

I was working for a client at their head office in a simple, old-fashioned building. There was no cafeteria, no fancy facilities to pamper employees. But we had a family of Pandas staying with us. Not real animals but soft toys that looked like baby pandas. I remember during my first week I did not realize what had happened but a Panda (small soft toy) flew at me and hit me on my back. I looked back to see who it was and everyone seemed to focus on their work. It wasn't just someone having fun at work, but my line manager. He ordered them online for the team and they were used as tools to have fun at the office.

Having worked for bigger MNCs, it seemed absolutely stupid to me and I pretty much questioned these ways of working. Few weeks on and I was beginning to become part of the fun, it felt good to chuck a panda at someone, a colleague who is now a friend and everyone is laughing along while working in an otherwise high-pressured environment where we were always delivering more than we thought we could. Just imagine, chucking a soft toy at your line manager. Sounds cheesy but it created a different vibe at work.

Another Monday, I came into office and found I was unable to move my mouse, and it dawned on me that someone had used a very strong tape we called the 'gorilla tape!' and stuck my mouse to the desk. I was angry and frustrated, I had so much to do and who would have time for these tricks when we are all under so much pressure. I did not bother much, removed the tape and carried on my work. But in a few weeks, I relented to the temptation of applying the same trick to my neighbour's desk. Fun was our way to deal with pressure.

The list of tricks we played on each other was endless, but our spirit to deliver projects was equally strong. Maybe it was the laughter we had at workplace every day that made us come to work.

## Game of Thrones

2017 *Game of Thrones*, Season 7

Person A: Where are you going?

Person B: To other side of the wall. Winter is coming.

Person A: To meet the white walkers?! Do you need any help?

Person B: No, I think I will be okay. I have my valyrian steel sword with me.

For those who don't watch *Game of Thrones,* you can skip the next few lines; for others, this wasn't a scene from *Game of Thrones.* I am the person B as a business consultant and Person A was my project manager. The other side of the wall was the second office building of the client I was working with and the white walkers were the tough business stakeholders we had. And when I said winter is coming, it was nothing but an escalation that we were dealing with. The valyrian steel was the work I had done to manage the expectation around mitigating the escalation.

This fun conversation could have been a stressful one had we chosen to use other realistic words. Instead of talking about how 'stressful the escalation' has been and how much 'work went into trying to mitigate' the escalation, or how much I 'hated those stakeholders', imagining them as white walkers somewhat did the trick and removed the stress.

This for me was the simple version of fun at work. Let me change a word here, fun 'while' working. We were not pulling fun at anyone and even if it seemed like that it was purely a coincidence. The understanding to use the *Game of Thrones* plot to explain ongoing business issues took away the stress from the crisis and brought creativity into play.

Questions for the readers:

1. Do you remember having fun while working?
2. Do you have fun now while working?

# The Solution Matrix

While laughter at the workplace is therapeutic, it is important to look at the framework prescribed by the Indian performing arts and consider the appropriateness of laughter-generating behaviour at the workplace to maintain decorum and still maintain positive vibes. The Indian performing arts classify three classes of people and their characteristic behaviour. For example, people with the Adhama (lower level) bent of mind may encourage ribald jokes in a professional forum without being mindful of the fact that they may potentially cause offence to some colleagues. People with the Madhyama (ordinary) mindset would be likely to behave like ordinary human beings who do get amused by slapstick and may laugh at a colleague's behaviour without realizing the potential offence caused. People with the Uttama mindset (people with outstanding wisdom and dignity) would only resort to indulgent smiles and never resort to 'completely letting themselves go' in public.

| Vibhav (Cause) | Sthahi Bhav (Dominant Emotion) | Anubhava (Experience)[1] | Vyabhichari (Related Emotions) | Response | | |
|---|---|---|---|---|---|---|
| | | | | Uttama (high) | Madhyama (medium) | Adhama (low) |
| Sensation of Joy | Laughter | Whooping noise, bodies release hormones and chemicals that have positive effects on our system | Relief, joy, happiness | Wide smile, restrained laughter | Loud laughter, sharing of harmless jokes | Guffaws, back slapping, slapstick humour at the expense of other people's shortcomings, smirking at someone's failure |

Apply 'A' framework:

| 1 | Acknowledge | Laugher does not need acknowledgement. It is the easiest emotion to express. In fact, often it is on autopilot mode and just flows out. Ever been in a situation where you wanted to control your laugher but you couldn't? Now, ever been in a situation where you should have controlled your laughter and were finding it hard? The situation is comical and critical at the same time. You would want to laugh when your boss makes a silly error, but you would not dare do it in front of him. This is why you need to acknowledge when you feel the need to chuckle at something. And a quick sense check to analyse what is the next step. |
|---|---|---|

(continued)

---

[1] See *https://www.laughteronlineuniversity.com/10-hormones-happiness/* (accessed on 22 April 2018).

(continued)

| 2 | Analyse | This step will help you understand if there is a reason not to laugh or not just react at that time. Ever felt like laughing when you know that someone you don't like at your workplace had been reprimanded for something or had resigned? It's always good to stop and reflect if that is the time to laugh about it or maybe drop the idea all together. |
| 3 | Accept | Laughter is a tricky one to manage. When someone feels the intense need to laugh, they will laugh. But at times when one knows that it is not the right time to laugh or get cracking on that joke just yet, it is important to accept the state your body wants to be in and let the feeling pass away or look for something to replace. It could be a smirk or trying to look at the serious side of things. Looking at things from other's perspective often helps. |
| 4 | Administer | If the case is otherwise, where it should be a laughing matter but not at that time and moment, it should be replaced with a different emotion and one should carefully choose what needs to be done. How about just saying 'I know this might be funny, but I do see the serious side.' |
| 5 | Act | Acting is doing. Not controlling but going with the laughter or expressing that you feel funny about the situation but you are also aware that it is not a laughing matter for that moment. |

# Benefits of Humour at Work

Here are some reasons why humour at workplace is important:

1.  **Being human**
    Humour is being human. As kids, we learn to cry and laugh and everything in between is a set of beliefs that created all other emotions. Leaning into laughter to take some stress off at the workplace is always a good idea. Laughter is and will be the best medicine.

2.  **Humour is like a vacuum cleaner**
    Humour helps looks at people and situations from different perspectives. Humour, at times, helps clear the air. It acts like a vacuum cleaner and clears out the dust in a relationship. While discussing a business-critical issue, a one-line joke between people who are trying to resolve it diffuses the pressure and resets everyone's thought process to get more creative.

3. **Humour heals**

   Humour is healing in its nature as well. A tough day at office, feeling stressed in a meeting, dealing with a tough situation—thinking or sharing a joke can help regain control over emotions.

4. **Humour is across all levels**

   Humour does not adhere to line management structures. A CEO sharing a laugh with any subordinate can break the glass ceiling and when a subordinate shares a joke back it builds a bond. Being laughed at and laughing with your team is an awesome experience and indicates an evolved level of leadership.

# Introducing Humour at the Workplace

Here are some no- or low-cost ideas to introduce humour at the workplace. For this emotion, rather than focussing at an individual level, the focus can be on building a 'smiling' environment at work.

1. **Digital newsletter**

   Create and distribute non-work digital newsletters which are created and delivered by everyone. Sometimes seeing the funny side of someone that you might not particularly like helps you to see the human side you otherwise may not see because of the role they are in.

2. **Decorate the workplace**

   Decorating the workspace during festivals is often done in businesses. There are businesses that are taking on a clean-desk policy, but nothing beats the joy of a person when he/she is allowed to express one's individuality through decorating a desk or a bay. Someone might want to put a picture of their family by the desk to remind them of why they work hard. Someone might want to put a small emblem of their favourite football team to get the spirit to win in them. Yet, others, may want to use colours that keep their spirits high.

3. **Wall of fame**
   One of my clients had a wall that was decorated with branches, leaves and golden apples. And people gave feedback to each other which were then pasted on to the branches. As people accumulated positive feedback, they were 'upgraded' to leaves and apples. And the one who got apples won significant rewards. They had a 'bird' as the biggest prize to the one who got maximum positive comments. This may sound very fluffy but becomes intense when people are trying to figure out who is giving feedback and who is not or why are they not getting feedback.

4. **Toys at work**

   > *We are under a lot of pressure and toys are our comfort. We need them like Linus needs his blanket.*
   >
   > —Mary Owen

   I remember how the stress levels optimized while I was working for one of my clients as the playfulness with the beach ball and soft panda toys made work fun.

5. **Pizza during project peak times**
   Imagine a day where there is a massive project meant to go live and the whole team is focused on delivering

the project. Ordering pizzas so they don't have to worry about lunch and the short conversation that happens while everyone is digging into the pizza together is an absolute winner to get some laughter.

6. **Mad meetings**
   These are meetings without any agenda, but fun. Get a team into a room and everyone should learn something new. Get smartphones out and play the same game to see who scores the most or get some balls and everyone learns how to juggle. Get in some Lego bricks and try to make a massive structure.

7. **Get rid of the riddle**
   Put up a riddle on a white board every week and whoever solves it first gets a reward.

8. **Game room**
   Set up a game room. Wii, PlayStation, Xbox, foosball, table tennis—that room where 100 per cent fun is guaranteed.

9. **Lean into the mischief**
   Mischief at work can be good as long as lines are not crossed—a simple prank (nothing that would result in HR calling you please) or any antics that brings laughter around. If unsure of what kind of fun is alright, lean into others for ideas to see where the bar is set.

10. **Pub meetings**
    Something I have experienced, why not call in a meeting with a proper office agenda in a nearby pub/coffee shop where work and celebration happens at the same time.

11. **Outdoor sessions**

One of the key contributors to stress building up at the workplace is the monotony of the closed environment and restrictive views. Weather and infrastructure permitting, a meeting or training session outdoors does wonders to introduce the fun element at the workplace!

## The laughter therapy—Jose's story

Jose, the Head of Human Resources of a large corporation, was entrusted with the entire gamut of people management responsibility. He was in the thick of corporate pressure—complaints from business heads about recruitment shortfall, attrition of talent during the industry boom—there was enough to speed up the greying at his temples. To add to his woes, were the undercurrents of non-alignment between the two people he reported to. In the tussle between the strong line of reporting and dotted line of reporting, Jose's bandwidth was severely stretched.

What kept Jose going through these tough years was his incorrigible sense of humour. Once, The Head of Marketing Communication, Ali, and Jose had been reprimanded by their top bosses over a half-page recruitment advertisement that had appeared in the morning newspaper. One of the top bosses was a Marketing Guru and believed he should have had the last word on anything creative that went out of the stable. The other top boss was responsible for numbers—revenue, profitability and the people who got these done. He believed company image had little to do with ads.

On a crisp Monday morning, Jose and Ali were summoned to the senior management floor. The two men on their mission ascended the wide staircase in unison. On the landing, they made eye contact—it was clear the bosses were not going to meet each other. Jose pointed his index finger at Ali and moved it to the right—Cabin no 1. Then, he pointed the index finger at himself and then moved it to the left—Cabin no 2. He then raised all 10 fingers, his watch and the landing. The two parted and returned to the landing in 10 minutes as planned. One had heard a blast on aesthetics and their absence in the company, the other had heard sarcastic references to style over substance. They were beat and exhausted by the effort and had left the cabins suitably sombre and chastised.

They walked down in unison and stepped out into the green grass of the company's picturesque campus. It was then that Jose uttered these historic words:

'When Elephants make love or war, it is the grass that gets trampled. Today, I'm feeling like the grass...'

Their somber faces gave way to peals of laughter and they strode back to their desks with a spring in their step!

## Reference

McGhee, Paul. 2012. 'Humour Helps Produce an Emotionally Intelligent Workplace.' www.laughterRemedy.com (accessed on 2 June 2017).

# Disgust

# The Manifestation of Disgust

As per our survey,

- Over 94 per cent of respondents have felt strong emotion at the workplace.
- Over 52 per cent reported trouble managing emotion at the workplace.
- Over 30 per cent reported feeling disgust as the trigger to leaving a job.
- Over 60 per cent reported feeling anger as the emotion that triggered separation from a job (anger which would eventually lead to disgust and the desperate need to go away from the situation).
- Only 5 per cent felt that they have leveraged disgust to enhance productivity.

## Depicting 'Disgust' in the Arts

The predominant emotional mood of disgust (*bibhatsa* as defined in the Indian arts) has several transitionary/temporary emotions associated with it. In Indian classical dance or theatre, the expression of 'disgust' is usually depicted with lips turned outwards, edges drooping down, eyes are narrowed, trembling, and the hands, arms, shoulders purposefully pulled away from the object causing disgust. The body language depicting the 'moving away from the situation' is of prime importance as the core of disgust is 'revulsion'.

## 'Disgust' in Science

Biologically, disgust is one manifestation of the well-known 'flight' response of the body when faced with a negative object/situation. When the body is faced with something deeply repulsive, such as putrid food, blood, injury, vermin-infected live or dead beings, severe deformity or human waste, foul smell or any other, the natural body reaction is to 'fight or flight'. The flight response is predominant and the body turns away, the nose turns up to minimize the intense bad smell. However, when the body is compelled to stay on in the negative situation and fight, the revulsion emerges in different ways. The natural reaction to a deeply disgusting sight or smell could be throwing up (the body is revolting and is unable to digest ingested food) or fainting as oxygen is diverted from the brain to other parts of the body trying to tackle the negative situation. Other responses to disgust could be screaming, copious crying or other signs of hysteria.

## Depicting 'Disgust' at the Workplace

Disgust is an extreme emotion and could also be the result of conditioning of the body and mind. The key reason it is so strong is that it is often a culmination of negative events/actions/triggers built up over several weeks/months and in some cases years. 'Disgust' would then be a result of one or all the three prolonged emotional moods of (a) fear (b) anger and/or (c) sadness. Among the transient/temporary emotions leading to disgust would be insult, shame, frustration, the feeling of being trapped, pressurized or any other negativity.

This would be especially true if it has not been possible to express any of these deep-felt emotions due to societal norms or to conform to, what we call in the modern-day workplace context, the acceptable social behaviour. When we apply the 'flight or fight response' to the modern workplace, it is evident that the 'flight' could only be a change of role, change of job or quitting. When the person who is disgusted with a situation is forced to stay on due to circumstances, the 'fight' response kicks in. Given workplace norms, it is not acceptable to exhibit certain behaviours which may otherwise be considered a natural response such as shouting and weeping. The emotion of disgust then gets relegated to a pile of pent-up resentment.

## Disgust at the workplace—Nisha's story

18 November 2014, London.

It was Nisha's fourth year at Premium Learning Solutions. As she read the latest email from Lauren, it was as if something snapped from within. Nisha shot an email to the entire team, reiterating the role of her own team and once again requesting Lauren and others to not circulate emails pertaining to her department without keeping her in the loop. Minutes after Nisha's group email hit his email box, her colleague Sean forwarded it to their boss vacationing without internet access. Once again, it hit Nisha how cornered she was—despite his insight into Lauren's manipulative tactics, Sean had chosen to be 'proactive' in reporting that nothing was wrong.

Just a few weeks before, a little tipsy Sean had asked Nisha why she was still around at Premium. It was a rare after-work social occasion when Nisha had been invited to join the team to step out. The social norms set by Lauren (and followed by the team for fear of being socially ostracized themselves) were clear—Nisha was not to be invited to any impromptu team lunches and drinks. So much so that as the team indulged in the bi-daily ritual of making everyone's teas and coffees in the pantry, nobody was to ask Nisha if she would like a beverage too. Nisha had endured this and more, dismissing the pettiness for what it was and telling herself repeatedly that her life was bigger than this rabbit hole. So, when that email from Lauren hit her email box, she should have been prepared—to ignore yet another attempt to take control of her job, her department. Instead, something that stirred within Nisha was far beyond the emotions she had experienced so far. Courtesy the petty politics unleashed by Lauren right from Nisha's first day on the job, Nisha had been grappling with the 'fear of being rejected' at her first assignment in a new country, 'angry' at the blatant disrespect and 'sad' that she could not quit as she needed the job for the mortgage. On the night of 18 November, Nisha collapsed, sobbing into her pillow into the wee hours of the morning.

On 19 November, she woke up, a listless version of herself, incapable of getting herself dressed and on the train to work.

For the next 30 days, the normally enthusiastic, responsible professional who took immense pride in the quality of work she delivered, made the most of her employer's work-from-home policy. She answered emails, pushed herself to be on the few conference calls that others initiated and did the bare minimum possible to chug along and finish what was started. Normally conscientious, the ignitor of projects, the monitor of work in progress and the finisher of otherwise dormant projects, Nisha simply did not care. Despite the loving family around her, Nisha would frequently end up curled up in bed, the tears refusing to let up. Usually the social animal just waiting for a reason to get a bunch of friends together, she cancelled social engagements that she had initiated and planned to precision, afraid that her friends would notice the vacant apathy in her eyes. During her moments of normalcy, Nisha expressed a desperate cry for help to her partner. During these moments of normalcy, she hated herself for putting her children through her bouts of apathy and weeping.

So, what was wrong with Nisha? During one such bout of normalcy, Nisha dragged herself to a job interview, carefully masking her dark circles with concealer make-up and dressed in a smart business suit to demonstrate to her prospective employers that she was what she had been for years—a dependable professional with a positive mindset. Exhausted by the train journey she took after long, she then dragged herself to a general physician, confessing that she was depressed. Pat came the diagnosis from the doctor who gave her pills to pop dismissing her as 'someone who was depressed due to London's cold, dreary weather'. While the diagnosis of depression was right, the reason attributed to it was wrong and the solution—a packet of anti-depressant pills—was completely wrong!

As Nisha's colleague Sean rightly pronounced, there was nothing new about the latest attempt and it was that very sameness that led to Nisha's extreme emotion of disgust—having repeatedly managed her other three negative emotions of fear, sadness and anger for four long years with no end in sight.

For those who knew Nisha, especially at her workplace, she had 'cracked up'. What does this 'cracking up' mean in medical terms? So how could Nisha have handled it?

# The Solution Matrix—3-DEM Applied to Disgust

As we established, the answer to managing emotion lies in the confluence of the following three: (a) the arts (b) management science (c) medical science.

What the arts say:

In Nisha's case, disgust led to depression. In other cases, it could lead to extreme anger, violence or any other behaviour considered 'highly impractical and inappropriate' in 'normal' circumstances. Disgust is a result of extreme provocation and the emergent action is of revulsion. As per the *Navrasa* theory, the state of the *rasa* manifests due to the cause or trigger of the emotion (*vibhav*), the effect of the emotion is the *anubhava* and the transient/related emotions are the *vyabhichari*.[1] While *rasas* demote the mood, these *bhavas* (associated with each *rasa*) create the mood through physical media—the brain, body or action.

| Vibhav (Cause) | Sthahi Bhav (Dominant Emotion) | Anubhava (Experience) | Vyabhichari (Related Emotions) | Response | | |
|---|---|---|---|---|---|---|
| | | | | *Uttama* (high) | *Madhyama* (medium) | *Adhama* (low) |
| Unwanted circumstance, insult | Disgust | Revulsion | Frustration, fear, anger | Walking away, polished communication, expressing displeasure without causing a scene | Strong words | Shouting, physical violence, door slamming, public scene to attract attention |

---

[1] http://onlinebharatanatyam.com/2008/09/11/the-cause-and-effect-of-rasa-sutra/

What science says:

In Nisha's case, prolonged negative emotions and the inability to change the situation had led to disgust and depression. But disgust need not always lead to depression. When the disgusted individual walks out/successfully changes the situation, it could lead to a feeling of liberation, relief or even euphoria. If the expression of disgust has occurred in a highly explosive manner resulting in collateral damage of relationships/practicalities pertaining to financial difficulty arising out of job loss, loss of face or loss of reputation, it could result in regret. Depending on the circumstances leading to the feeling and then expression of disgust, there would be a 'temporary' change in endocrine levels. If these changes are temporary and event-driven, things would settle down after the situation is corrected.

However, depending on the severity of the circumstances leading to disgust and the longevity of the unchangeable negative situation, the body's response may take much longer to revert to the normal and in some cases, may never come back.

If disgust does result in depression, the body displays hormonal imbalances.[2] A possible mechanism is a default in the hypothalamic-pituitary-adrenal (HPA) axis—the system that manages the body's response to stress. When a person perceives a frightening situation, the hypothalamus amplifies the production of substances such as corticotrophin-releasing factor (CRF). These substances then stimulate the pituitary gland to release various hormones that prepare the body for a 'fight or flight' response.

---

[2] http://www.healthcommunities.com/depression/endocrine-system_jhmwp.shtml

Chronic activation of the HPA axis may contribute to depression. Indeed, depressed patients often exhibit higher blood levels of stress hormones than those who are not depressed.

# Management Science and Disgust

In management terms, Nisha had demonstrated 'fragility'; an otherwise strong individual had broken down physically and emotionally following prolonged, repeated blows to her self-esteem.

When a person opens his mind to the fact that no workplace will ever be perfect, the emotion toolbox described further becomes easy to practice (Figure 8.1).

To better understand why the workplace had such a deep impact on Nisha, let us delve into one of the most popular of management theories—the 'Hierarchy of Needs' by Abraham Maslow, also popularly known as Maslow's pyramid (Figure 8.2) (Martin and Joomis 2007, 72–75).

Psychologist Abraham Maslow identified five categories of basic needs common to all people. Maslow represented these needs as a hierarchy in the shape of a pyramid. According to Maslow, individuals must meet the needs at the lower levels of the pyramid before they can successfully be motivated to tackle the next levels. The lower levels represent deficiency needs and the upper levels represent growth needs. Growth needs can never be satisfied completely.

Contrary to the deficiency needs, for which motivation diminishes when a need is satisfied, as growth needs are met, people's motivation to meet them increases.

For example, the more one comes to understand, the more one's motivation to learn more increases. For Maslow, once a

Figure 8.1   The Outcome Expected When We Successfully Manage Emotions

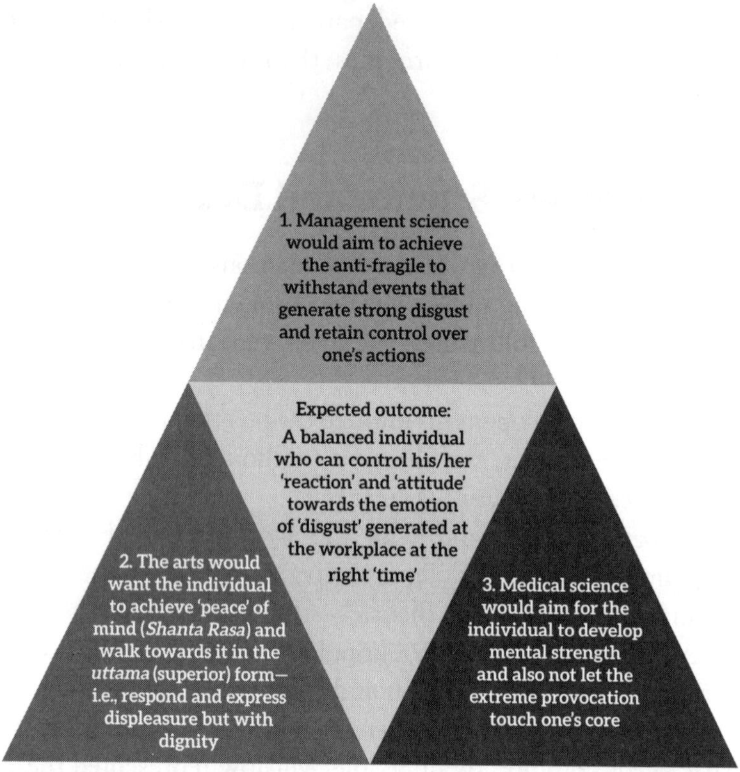

**1.** Management science would aim to achieve the anti-fragile to withstand events that generate strong disgust and retain control over one's actions

Expected outcome:
A balanced individual who can control his/her 'reaction' and 'attitude' towards the emotion of 'disgust' generated at the workplace at the right 'time'

**2.** The arts would want the individual to achieve 'peace' of mind (*Shanta Rasa*) and walk towards it in the *uttama* (superior) form— i.e., respond and express displeasure but with dignity

**3.** Medical science would aim for the individual to develop mental strength and also not let the extreme provocation touch one's core

*Source:* Authors.

need was met, it disappeared as the individual moved on to the next level.

Maslow (1968) estimated that less than 1 per cent of adults achieve total self-actualization. Recent academic research reinventing Maslow's age-old famous pyramid, question the presence of self-actualization in the hierarchy in the first place.

According to the researchers questioning the holistic application of Maslow's pyramid, the top of the new pyramid are

**Figure 8.2**　Maslow's Hierarchy of Needs

Self-actualization

Self-esteem

Love and belonging

Safety and security

Sustainance

*Source:* Maslow (1968).

three evolutionarily critical motives that Maslow overlooked—mate acquisition, mate retention and parenting.[3]

The researchers state in the article that while self-actualization is interesting and important, it isn't an evolutionarily fundamental need. Instead, many of the activities that Maslow labelled as self-actualizing (e.g., artistic creativity) reflect more biologically basic drives to gain status, which in turn serve the goal of attracting mates.

This brings us to a very interesting dimension of a person's primary motivation to go to work. At a stage of one's life when the primary motivation for life has no connection with a

---

[3] https://asunqw.asu.edu/content/maslows-pyramid-gets-much-needed-renovation

professional goal (for instance, seeking a partner or parenting), the importance of work as a source of happiness is reduced and, in fact, put into perspective. In the case of Nisha, though, a fulfilling and full life as a partner in a happy marriage and parent in positive family relationships was not enough. This is probably because of her pursuit of self-actualization as well as her past experiences of having sought and realized happiness from the workplace. Nisha, at this point, did not realize and acknowledge that she was an exception.

In arriving at a solution for Nisha and helping her reach her anti-fragile state, following is another framework proposed by the authors of this book—'the 4Ws and the How'.

## Analysing Disgust: The 4 Ws and the How

| 'Why' was Nisha working | She was seeking self-actualization but had no choice except working to fulfil a lower need (of earning enough to cover her mortgage). |
|---|---|
| 'What' should she have aimed for | Nisha should have stopped expecting happiness from her workplace and only assigned it the level of importance it deserved—as a source of income to fulfil her 'deficiency need' of income. |
| 'Where'/'When' | She should have acknowledged the lowered importance of the workplace in her life within the first 90 days after beginning her job instead of waiting for 4 years and then cracking up and asserting herself at the workplace to stem the bullying. |
| 'How' | She should have:<br><br>• Laid the boundaries of the number of hours she would work.<br>• Applied the 5A framework and practised emotional fasting to ensure that the negative forces at the workplace did not invade her personal mental space beyond work hours.<br>• Sought self-actualization outside the workplace. |

How can you apply the 5A framework?

How could Nisha have dealt with the extreme emotion of disgust? The answer is by applying the 5As framework.

| | | | | |
|---|---|---|---|---|
| 1 | Acknowledge | I am not perfect and nor are my co-workers. There will be occasions when strong emotions will be generated at the workplace. | I am feeling something. And the feeling is.... | Negative. It is 'disgust' |
| 2 | Analyse | It will help to put into categories what I'm really feeling (see the nine emotions) and understand at least some of what happens in the brain. | What has led me to feel this way? | The repeated actions of my colleagues to not accept me, to undermine my presence leading to anger at being insulted, sadness at not being accepted and fear for not being able to pay my mortgage if I quit my job |
| 3 | Accept | Whatever emotion is generated, in most cases, I will not have control over the perpetuator of those emotions. | Every time one of my colleagues says or does anything to me, I am bound to feel disgusted. | I need to either change my colleagues (beyond my control), change my job (fear of mortgage) or change myself. |
| 4 | Administer | I will 'choose' my attitude. | As changing my colleagues or job at this stage is practically not possible, I need to have a plan of action to change myself. | The attitude I have chosen is of courage. |
| 5 | Act | I will 'follow' my plan. | Every time one of my colleagues does anything to make me sad or angry, I will not let the fear of losing my job take over. | I will tell myself that the PIG (explained in the following paragraph) is all right! |

Especially when one feels intense negative emotion at the workplace generated by a(/multiple) stakeholder(/s), the perspective of the PIG is useful (Morgan 1993). Each of us serves some value/utility to the individual stakeholders we deal with. Let's take the example of a pig and what the pig signifies in the life of each of its stakeholders. For a child, a pig could be a pretty pink animal in a picture book or an immense source of entertainment like 'Peppa Pig!' For a foodie with predominant carnivorous taste, it could just be the ham to be consumed as a source of nutrition. To a butcher, the pig could be a source of income. In the framework of certain religious beliefs, the pig is an animal to be kept away from—a symbol of the forbidden. For a child growing up on a farm, the pig could be a pet.

If you look at these relationships carefully, it is evident that the pig denotes various things to different people and nobody really cares about the feelings of the pig or about the pig's well-being except perhaps the person who has him as a pet and the pig's own family. Similarly, one can analyse one's utility in the eyes of each of our stakeholders at the workplace.

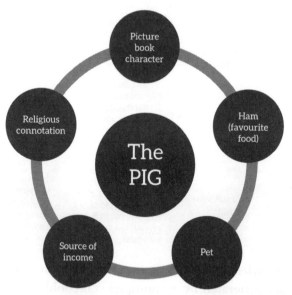

At Premium Learning Solutions, Nisha suffered sadness and anger for four years and finally acknowledged that she was just the ham. After her former boss Chris had moved on, she realized that no one else cared about Nisha's feelings as an individual. The realization that she was 'just the ham' hit hard especially after her commitment and pride in executing every job on target and with great passion. Nisha's collapse and her subsequent quitting of her job could have been handled better if she had applied the 3-DEM toolbox, the 5A framework and the pig analysis of stakeholder perception.

To walk towards her anti-fragile, the management science arm of the 3-DEM toolbox has the following explanation for Nisha:

If the pig is viewed by a butcher as just a piece of ham, that is due to the inherent limitations of the butcher's origins, background, lack of education and absence of worldview. Just because the butcher views the pig as a piece of flesh to be diced and ready for sale does not mean that the pig is not a complete animal. Irrespective of how the pig is viewed by the different stakeholders, the pig is still alright!

# References

Martin, D., and K. Joomis. 2007. *Building Teachers: A Constructivist Approach to Introducing Education*. Belmont, CA: Wadsworth.

Maslow, A. H. 1968. *Toward a Psychology of Well Being*. New York: D. Van Nostrand Company.

Morgan, G. 1993. *Imaginization: New Mindsets for Seeing, Organizing and Managing*. Newbury Park and San Francisco, CA: SAGE Publications.

Nohria, N., B. Groysberg, and L.-E. Lee. 2008. 'Employee Motivation.' *Harvard Business Review* 86 (7/8): 78–84.

# Wonder

*There are no seven wonders of the world in the eyes of a child. There are seven million.*
—Walt Streightiff

*Aasmaan hai neela kyun* [Why is the sky blue?]
*Pani geela geela kyun* [Why is the water wet?]
*Gol kyun hai zameen* [Why is the world round?]
*Silk mein hai narmi kyun* [Why is silk soft?]
*Aag mein hai garmi kyun* [Why is the fire hot?]
*Do aur do paanch kyun nahi*
[Why are two and two, not five?]
*Pedh ho gaye kam kyun* [Why have the trees reduced?]
*Teen hai yeh mausam kyun* [Why are there three seasons?]
*Chaand do kyun nahi* [Why don't we have two moons?]
*Duniya mein hai jung kyun* [Why is there war in the world?]
*Behta laal rang kyun* [Why does the red colour flow?]
*Sarhaden hai kyun har kahin*
[Why are there boundaries everywhere?]
*Socha hai yeh tumne kya kabhi*
[Have you ever thought about this?]
*Socha hai ki hai yeh kya sabhi*
[Have you ever thought what is all this?]
*Socha hai, socha nahi toh socho abhi*
[If not, then think about it now?]

This is a song from the Bollywood movie *Rock On!!* These
are questions we usually don't ask as adults. But once upon a
time as children, we were curious, we would ask and when
and if we did get the answers, we would look at those in
admiration, joy and wonder.

As a 3-year-old would ask on night drive: 'Daddy, why is
the moon following us everywhere?'

Because we often don't have the exact answer or we believe
the person asking the question does not have the capability
to understand the answer, we just don't answer or encourage
questions!

As children, we are naturally curious. When something unexpected happens, we express wonder and the joy that comes along, may it be the sight of a simple dandelion blowing out a spray of wondrous pink in the wind or touching a red button on a small plastic box that can switch on a world of visuals—a remote controlled TV set!

And this curiosity is what invokes learning and flags the beginning of the process of experiencing wonder. And once a person falls in love with what they discovered while being curious, they make it a part of their conscious mind and do more to learn or master whatever it is.

Toddlers learn quickly because they do everything out of curiosity. One could teach a 3-year-old how to clean his/her teeth properly by 'training' them or by arousing their 'curious' about brushing teeth. How do you do that? Get curious to make them curious. Get them a toothbrush with light, and they curiously play a game to see if it is possible to brush all the teeth before the light goes off.

When a toddler grows up, the curiosity gets overdrawn by learning and academics, and most of them stop learning and find the process boring as they are not curious about anything anymore.

When they become adults at the workplace, it becomes mostly about paying the bills, and the only curiosity is when a salary increase is on the cards—curious about how much will it go up.

How often do we encourage curiosity at the workplace? Or explore deep within our own mind and hearts about something?

We are talking about a positive sense of wonder at the workplace. Wonder is triggered by seeing something new and unexpected, a happy emotional mood with a mist of curiosity and surprise.

In our survey,

- Only 31 per cent people experience wonder at their workplace when every business is trying 100 per cent to delight their customers.
- 64 per cent people try and leverage on curiosity to boost productivity.

## Wonder in the Arts

Wonder or amazement takes you beyond the obvious, beyond the mechanical, mundane aspect of work. It demands belief in the extraordinary and the passion to pursue it and make it happen. In classical dance, the protagonist experiencing wonder is either kneeling or leaning slightly, arms outstretched or limp on either side, the palms upturned, the fingers uncurled as if questioning the magic of the Universe that made this miracle possible. The eyes are wide open, the tears of joy/ admiration at the brink. In the highly-dramatized versions of the arts, the eyebrows are twitching.

## Wonder Explained in Science

While the awe that we experience triggers joy, delight and the happiness chemicals (dopamine, oxytocin), it also lends itself to helping us feel humbler, making us feel smaller in comparison with the overwhelming, larger-than-life situation (Piff and Keltner 2015). A 2012 Stanford University study found the clinical benefits of the feeling of awe and concluded that it helps enhance compassion and empathy, essentials at the workplace.

**Figure 9.1**   The Path to Experiencing Wonder

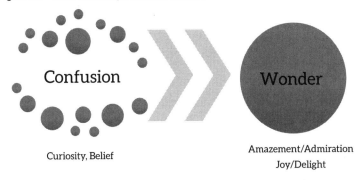

Confusion

Wonder

Curiosity, Belief

Amazement/Admiration
Joy/Delight

Awe has been described as a culmination of many emotions and the feeling of awe also inspires people to collaborate/ help others and demonstrate compassion (Piff et al. 2015). Interestingly, the depiction of awe in the arts shows that the person who is awestruck is diminished in physical size before a larger-than-life imagery of the object/person who is the focal point of the wonder. Science too appears to support the same with studies showing that people who experience awe show decreased narcissism and entitlement and more pro-social behaviour (Schultz 2012).

What could be in the way of experiencing amazement? Lack of receptivity, cynicism, lack of curiosity, inability to look outside a set framework, refusal to learn/be impressed/ refusal to admit to one's emotions.

What could be the possible occasions to feel wonder/ amazement/awe at the workplace? It could be when

- Someone accomplishes something beyond one's expect-ations.
- A goal/target that seemed impossible to achieve is fulfilled.

- A vision that was sometimes too ridiculous to even be articulated is realized.
- A relationship that was only going downhill was salvaged.
- Witnessing unexpected beauty in a person/situation.

Why do we love holidays so much? It is so because there is a curiosity to visit a new place or do something new. With the systemization at work, it is difficult.

There is massive change in the way people used to be curious at work or in life. Before the age of the internet, it was a known small world. There was so much to be curious about. Search engines didn't exist to answer curious questions in the fraction of a second. One had to struggle, take some actions and wait to really get to the answer. Being curious was fun.

Then the bulb was invented, cars were on the road, the telephone to talk and people got used to conforming to a very systematic life.

And today, the generation that went through the systemization does not bother with being curious.

Among entrepreneurs, there is a mad rush to come up with the next big idea like those of Airbnb, Uber or Amazon. So many young people came up with a genius app or website. The distinction was they were curious about something that led them to a big find, while others are busy trying to find a niche or fill up a gap in the market.

## Why Has This Curiosity Diminished?

Curious people are easy to identify but difficult to find:

- They ask questions.
- They love surprises.
- They listen without any judgement.

- They have high awareness levels.
- They are willing to make mistakes.
- They are not scared to ask silly questions.
- They are keen on the future.

Think of a time when you held back, when you thought you had a question and left it to ask a specific person later or maybe to figure it out on your own later.

Think of a time when you did not speak up about a suggestion with a fear that you might be judged or maybe you were hearing someone and chose not to listen because of biases you had against the person.

Only a curious mind can be learning forever.

Being curious about new places, people and perspectives makes the circle of learning bigger. A curious mind can find new avenues for learning (Juliana 2016).

# How Hungry Are You with Curiosity?

## Curiosity Needs the Right Set of Environments to Grow

A straightjacketed school education system with so many students crammed into a classroom demands that students sit quietly and listen to the professor. There is no space for curiosity.

## The professor's story

Even as his counterparts prepared students for exams that would in turn lead them to high-paying campus offers, a professor decided to approach his class differently. On Day 1 of his MBA class, he declared,

'If you want me to read the book, then you have wasted the fee you have paid as you could have paid few hundred bucks for the book and read it on your own. If you don't challenge what I teach, you are again wasting your money, because the fee you have paid to the college is funding my salary. And as customers, you ought to challenge me and make sure I come well prepared every time.'

He made his students curious by giving a high-level definition of a topic which was then discussed by the students among themselves, challenging their thinking.

Cut to a corporate setting, there are professionals sitting in a workshop meant for brainstorming. What really happens is everyone is sitting still and quietly staring at a PowerPoint presentation. People are used to sitting still, whereas curiosity grows when there is movement.

Ever been in a CEO's update where the senior leadership team stands in front of all its employees to give a quarterly or annual update. When it comes to Q&A, how many questions come up? How hard-hitting are those questions? The quantity and quality of the questions will reflect on the room for curiosity that exits in the workplace.

And all questions that come up increase brain activity, helping feel wonder!

**Learning curiosity takes practice.** It is not merely a matter of asking loads of questions. It's asking the right question at the right time. Sometimes you could ask 10 questions and not get anywhere and feel as if you are swimming in an endless ocean. Sometimes you ask a single question, and that is all it takes.

**When you ask new questions that make you feel uncomfortable, new doors open.** When curious, the mind opens. And sometimes you get interested in things otherwise you wouldn't be. During his days at university, Steve Jobs chose to attend calligraphy classes simply out of curiosity. We also know how the same curiosity was used and the beautiful sources were born on the Mac.

We are often so busy living in fear that we miss some awesome things that we never knew existed. People are offered free sessions on so many interesting themes and areas of life. But often people avoid availing of anything advertised as 'free' as they are suspicious that it is a pitch to sell them something. Of course, there will be a pitch to sell something, but it is also a case of remembering that we have the power to say 'No'. Even better, saying 'No' does not require any special power. We leave out so many things we could have listened and learned about through curiosity and give in to the fear of being sold.

**New facts new idea.** Curiosity is all about looking at something in a holistic way multiple times and finding something new. How often do you feel so?

'I know this report/system/business at the back of the hand.' It's a big assumption, and what we are trying to imply is I am not curious anymore? Why not be on the hunt for something new in that business or report you never knew before?

Certain personalities in the workplace are otherwise in a lazy zone, refusing to be curious, refusing to experience wonder and still doing well for themselves. It's when they get hit with an issue; they get off like a road racer. It's the curiosity of the unknown that drives them. In their core area and know-it-all zone, they have encountered something they have never heard before. They become curious and start driving high performance in search of a breakthrough. Curiosity helps them get to the answer. Despite their own closed minds refusing to welcome curiosity and the resultant wonder, majority choose to still not accept the unknown and blame it on someone else and that their world is perfect.

**Curiosity opens new doors.** Some people thrive under pressure. And sometimes great things happen when a person is faced with a major deadline. There is obvious stress, but there is a choice to be scared and use fear to complete the goal at hand. Or use wonder and curiosity to do it with a sparkle. Most entrepreneurs are created by situations in which they have to take some risks that they did not choose to face—fear or not having money to pay the bills, family home mortgage and other stuff. In the process, they often either give up and go back to a 9–5 job or become curious to create some magic. Curiosity thrives when it is challenged and when we are on edge. Steve Jobs although had many challenges while creating the Apple brand, it all started with curiosity, curious to know what the customer does not know and to challenge the status quo.

**Bonded between teams.** '#oneteam' seems to be the mantra every workplace is singing about. How do you achieve a true 'one team' spirit at all levels of management? Curiosity can work magic in relationships. When teams don't just work together but are truly curious to help each other out or to find out common interests through exploration—baking competitions, pub nights and playing pranks on each other at the office!—the one who was curious to play and be a part of the 'gang' bonded—Curious to know who will bake what for the baking day and curious to find more activates to do together. If two people in a team don't get along, sometimes a spar of curiosity can bring them together. The two people may not get along but may find out that they both have a common interest in something such as wine tasting, sailing or something that can initiate that first step towards becoming a one-team.

Isn't that what dating is all about?: curiosity to find out common interest in the other person to get a conversation going.

## Stories of curiosity leading to wondrous creations

- Dr Gautam Bhan was curious to understand the lack of affordable housing in one of most populated countries in the world. His curiosity led him to a belief that we need to change our attitude towards slum dwellers and give them their right to call their place 'basti'. He was curious about how, instead of demolishing, the existing small houses could be created into better homes for them.

- Shubhendu Sharma, an industrial engineer, moved away from making automobiles to start building forests in cities and developed about hundred jungles in 35 cities. His curiosity led him to discover that it takes less than the cost of an iPhone to convert a 6-space car park to a forest. The curiosity of creating a forest in cities helped him work with limited resources.

- Music composer Sneha Khanwalkar (featured in Bollywood movies such as Gangs of Wasseypur, Oye Lucky! Lucky Oye!) has created a virtual own zone whereby simply waving and with legs you can play different instruments.

- Manu Prakash was curious about making changes to the massive rural areas of India which lack basics like electricity. High curiosity leads him to create Foldscope–a paper micro-scope. This can be used to conduct a simple blood test in an area without any power requirements. His view is for everyone to start thinking of science, not as a tough subject to clear in exams, but a fun thing to explore and use right in our homes and kitchens.

- Is there anything productive about pollution? Anirudh Sharma, a young scientist, discovered that. He created the process of converting pollution into something productive. As he said, 'Pollution is nothing but resources not harvested.' His curiosity to get something productive out of pollution led him to convert that pollution into ink!

So be curious!

There is another elephant in the room that needs to be addressed. Rather a very curious one. Ever been in a meeting or a workshop where there is this one person who does not stop asking questions—the over curious one, who never stops asking questions.

## Hazel's story

Hazel was extremely curious with lots of questions. All her colleagues dreaded being her in any meetings or training courses. Hazel had 101 questions ready for everything. As much as Hazel enjoyed asking questions, she never realized how annoyed her colleagues were because of the number of questions she had. Meeting overran, training courses used to drag on. There are three perspectives to break down this situation. Three participants who can influence or be victimized with this over curious being in the mix:

1. Hazel herself. Who was aware of the stares being thrown at her because of her question, but she found it equally difficult to bottle her curiosity.

2. The person facing the questions: The person chairing the meeting was the one who had to answer the questions. It is easy to say, 'there are no silly questions'. Sometime answering them does take a lot of patience.

3. The ones who are sitting around: These are the other attendees who cannot bear another question and would like to be out of that room and go for that smoke break or whatever next interesting thing is on their mind.

Here are some tips you can use during a meeting or otherwise.

1. **Do-it-yourself approach:** For people who have too many questions, it's better to teach them how to fish rather than catch the fish for them. If you seem to be the go-to person, direct them to the original source where you would have got the answer from. It could be a help guide or may be a matter of a web search to get the answer.

2. **Use auto-responder:** If curious people are sending you questions over emails, use the auto responder. Instead of setting it only when you are out of office, get more creative with it. For an IT super user, a message could read 'Thanks for your email. Due to the high volume of email, there could be delay in responding to your email. If you query is about the new software, please refer to the help question. If that doesn't help, please raise a support ticket and someone will respond.'

3. **Create a frequently-asked–questions (FAQ) bank:** You can eliminate most of the questions people raise that are repetitive in nature or you find are slowing others down in a training workshop. Once you have a list of usual questions that come up, create an FAQ section and share it with the wider audience. This is where you put the silliest to the most burning questions. Send it out with the training material, meeting minutes and any digital format you can.

4. **Question limit:** Sometimes, curious people ask very perceptive questions. It's good to try and answer as much as you can but it is equally important to value your own and everyone's time—whether in training, meeting or when an over curious person comes to your desk. Set a rule. Make them aware that you can

only answer three questions as there is a lot more to cover or there are other more pressing tasks that you need to attend to. In special circumstances, you can set up a separate slot of time to catch up with those who need exclusive time, but no one should take you for granted.

## The wonder of transforming lives: Vilas Chaphekar's story

August 2018, Pune, India.

Fifty plus young children shriek in delight at the new experiences they are exposed to—a classical dance session, a game of tennis, Chinese food, a globe, a chessboard, a set of picture books. The wonder—these children have mothers forced to work in despicable surroundings and there is no news of their fathers. But today, these children are oblivious of these painful facts and are looking forward to school, homework, computers, birthdays and outings like others their age! This is awe-inspiring at a different level!

Having dedicated his life to social work through his social organization Vanchit Vikas, Vilas Chaphekar used to run a free school for street children near Ghatkopar railway station in Mumbai in the 1980s. Given the quality of education, the number of children grew to 150! He had no idea whose children these were. He then discovered that several of these were children of sex workers. Curiosity about the lives and challenges faced by this marginalized population led Chaphekar to the conclusion that all the mothers of these children had been forced into the sex trade at some stage of their lives.

Chaphekar's work did not stop with curiosity, and he delved deeper into the issues faced by these children—the mothers having to 'retire' early forcing little girls as young as 12 into the trade and the boys relegated to performing odd jobs, all of this in a highly demeaning and unhealthy environment. Chaphekar's curiosity was matched by a vision and a determined approach that many may had ridiculed at that time and several still hesitate to even applaud in public.

In 1989, Chaphekar and his associates at Vanchit Vikas, launched Nihar, a home for such children located in the outskirts of Pune. Nihar means 'dew drop'. As Chaphekar says,

'The dew drop looks beautiful on a deep green leaf. But it is always on shaky ground. If the leaf is ripped apart or withers away, the dew drop would mingle into the muck below. We need to preserve this innocence with care.'

Starting with 15 children, today 80 plus students have passed out of Nihar with stars like a boy who completed his doctorate, a manager in an IT company and several social workers and homemakers who are now engaged in salvaging the lives of others along with their families!

This is wonder, a direct example of curiosity followed by passionate pursuit and determined action!

## The Solution Matrix

There are two possible outcomes of extreme curiosity at the workplace. Curiosity, awe and the desire to envisage a future that no one else seems to see, could be termed as vision or mere rebellion and refusal to accept the status quo. It is only those who 'see' what is not obvious, work towards making the impossible happen. The framework defined in the Indian performing arts below helps us analyse this emotion and arrive at an appropriate response.

| Vibhav (Cause) | Sthahi Bhav (Dominant Emotion) | Anubhava (Experience) | Vyabhichari (Related Emotions) | Response |
|---|---|---|---|---|
| Curiosity, desire for a solution/ closure | Wonder | Curiosity tempts us, want to know more, pushing boundaries, feel it in the gut, increased activity in the brain to store memories | Happiness, feeling inspired or motivated | Makes memory stronger, helps focus |

## Applying 'A' framework:

| 1 | Acknowledge | When you feel an itch in your brain, when you are feeling something in the gut and are eager to know or do something, curiosity is kicking in. When you feel you are 100 per cent focused and you are 'in the game' and 'on the track', there is room for curiosity to grow. |
|---|---|---|
| 2 | Analyse | When you know your mind is buzzing with something to soak up and learn something new, it's time to slow down. Slowing down will help you analyse. How much do you slow down? Slow down so much that you are craving to speed up. It's creating that moment when you are thirsty and there is water in front of you. But you decide to count till 50 before you have a sip. |
| 3 | Accept | Slowing down is a step to accepting curiosity. Accepting is using tools that would help get the buzz out of the brain. Scribble on a paper to empty your mind's buzzing thoughts. Maybe say them aloud. It's like letting steam off so you can start again. Then administer the right questions to make most out of curiosity. |
| 4 | Administer | Administering curiosity is about playing with the idea. Taking a 360-degrees global view on the task at hand. It's like playing with Lego. How many pieces can you break the tasks into? What can you make of it? The good, bad, ugly outcomes you could get. Make a list till there is no space on the paper. Pick the top 3 and get to act on them. |
| 5 | Act | This is letting the curiosity disrupt the outside world. Take action on one chosen strategy that will help you live that curiosity and spread the feel of feeling wonder. There are questions listed further down the chapter to allow playing and act on curiosity. |

# Tools/Tips/Worksheets

- **Open to failure culture**
  To let curiosity thrive in the workplace, teams should be allowed to fail. Yes, there are business objectives to be met, but there is not just one perfect route to get there. People should be made aware that they can make mistakes and can try new things.

- **Allow new ways**
  There should be a culture to allow stuff done in ways it hasn't been done before. Try the unorthodox. Every team player should be given the opportunity to do things their own way. And then sync it all together. Allow working from home on Friday. Allow extended paternity leave to fathers. Allow parents to bring in their kids into workplace once every 90 days. These unusual ways of working open bonds between teams and will increase the trust at workplace leading to more avenue for curiosity to grow.

- **Take the good, the bad and the ugly in the same stride**
  There will be some disruption when you allow people to be curious in their own way. It's like letting a child go free in a toy store. And the management should be open to taking in the ideas in a positive stride. No matter how bad or ugly they are. Listen, learn and then give feedback. Curiosity demands change and change must be handled with an open mind.

- **Invite curious people**
  Invite guest speakers who bring curiosity to the workplace—doesn't matter which industry, background. It can be anyone who can demonstrate curiosity and open people's mind about being curious.

- **Do the opposite of what competition does**
  This is a very proactive way to encourage curiosity. It might mean leaning into your fears. Imagine if someone told you to drive in the opposite direction of the road towards oncoming traffic. What will your strategy be? Likewise, come up with a strategy that is opposite to what the competition is doing. Well it could succeed or fail miserably, so beware!

- **Minimum three perspectives**
  This is a golden principle that could be applied. Any issue, any solution will require being justified with at least three perspectives. We will take the example of changing the back end of a website; The three perspectives can be the impact it can have on IT, business and customers. Enforcing the rule to come up with at least three different views on anything strategic forces new roads to open.

- **Manage changing changes**
  Curiosity will lead to disruption and ever-changing changes. It opens doors for creativity to flood through and leads to many ideas being tried and tested. There must be a proactive plan to manage the ever-changing changes. There is a thin line between making changes out of curiosity and business changing its requirements by the second. A scope creep or change in requirement is okay if it is based on curiosity. If it is because the business is curious to know how the outcome will change, it will be based on being open to the change with everyone without any scaremongering.

- **Eureka ideas**
  Roll out an initiative. A new coin in the workplace called Eureka. Every time a person in the business

comes up with the idea that is truly awesome, give that person eureka coin. And link it to a reward system where based on the coins a team or a person will be rewarded. It will measure the curiosity levels in workplace and initiate healthy competition within to bring wonder in the workplace.

## Question Quotient

In a world that rewards conformity, it is relatively rare to encounter curiosity. When you do, it is important to not just retain this curiosity and awe, but also channelize it towards focussed and constructive activity. Consider asking the questions below.

1.  **I am wondering and curious to know**
    When you talk to colleagues and want them to explain something, don't just say the usual 'Tell me more' or 'Can you explain the details'. Our mind creates a distinction between every word we use. No matter how big or small the issue is, or how technical or non-technical, challenge yourself to use more curious words, 'I am wondering how we manage that in our IT system, I am curious to know more.' As much it is not appropriate to use corporate language at home, what if you tried using more emotive words in the workplace?

2.  **If you had magic wand, what would you see or do?**
    Whenever you find someone stuck with an issue, you have plans in place to mitigate issues—Plan A, Plan B and so on. What if we moved away from a list of plans and think in order? Instead, we draw no lines or

boundaries and let the subject matter expert be as creative as possible. Ask the question 'I know we have this issue or requirement but if you had a magic wand what would you do about the problem...?' Asking for Plan A introduces the pressure to come up with something that will work with the highest probability. Asking for the magic one can create, the person will dig deep in their instinct and come up with a solution.

3.  **What happens when you imagine?**
    Curiosity thrives where there are no rules to conform. Imagining needs a free mind. But how do you get your mind to think free when there is so much pressure of work and deadline? When brainstorming within self or with the team, using the right words can unlock the freedom.

4.  **How do you know?**
    Ever came across a manager/subordinate/colleague who is hell-bent on a statement they carry? 'This work-place has always been like this, full of politics with no consideration for employees' or 'If you want to go up the ladder, you have to please your manager and other seniors.' Ask them a simple question 'How do you know?' And give them some time to think before they answer—a pause to slow them down. And then get an answer. This is not about someone else but only that person. That person needs to be curious about where this belief comes from. When I am working with clients and they are telling me that everything is wrong in their workplace, I ask them the same question and leave them in their space for more than 5 minutes. Amazing, curious perspectives come up.

5.  **If you did know, what would be the answer?**
How do you turn fear into curiosity? Give the baton in the hand of the person who fears it the most. When you come across a fear that is engulfing your mind at the workplace, ask yourself 'If I did know, what would be the answer?' It opens a new perspective and often pushes fear in the background and makes way for curiosity.

> *We keep moving forward, opening new doors,*
> *and doing new things, because we're curious and*
> *curiosity keeps leading us down new paths.*

—Walt Disney

# References

Breines, Juliana. 2016, March 8. *Four Awe-inspiring Activities.* Berkeley, CA: Greater Good Science Center at UC Berkeley.

Piff, P., and D. Keltner. 2015, May 22. 'Awe?' *New York Times.*

Piff, P. K., P. Dietze, M. Feinberg, D. M. Stancato, and D. Keltner. 2015. 'Awe, the Small Self, and Prosocial Behavior.' *Journal of Personality and Social Psychology* 108 (6): 883–99. http://dx.doi.org/10.1037/pspi0000018

Schultz, Colin. 2012, July 31. 'How the Feeling We Call Awe Helped Humans Conquer the Planet.' *Smithsonian Magazine.*

CHAPTER
**10**

# Sorrow

*Heaven knows we need never be ashamed of our tears, for they are rain upon the blinding dust of the earth, overlying our hard hearts. I was better after I had cried than before—sorrier, more aware of my ingratitude, gentler.*
                    —Charles Dickens, *Great Expectations*

# Sorrow in the Arts

The traditional depiction of sorrow shows a face with drooping lips, eyes swollen due to a bout of weeping or tears rolling down. As is the case with laughter, some cultures are more open with displaying emotion than others. Besides, the differences in gender are most stark in the emotional mood of sorrow. Traditionally, women have been more 'permitted' to shed tears while several cultures even today are judgmental about men shedding tears and accusing them of being weak.

# Sorrow Explained by Science

Feeling low or sad means that the levels of opioids in the brain increase. Prolonged high levels of opioids could impact the immune system and enhance the risk of heart disease.

Every bout of sorrow is certainly not a sign of clinical depression.[1,2] But every time we feel sad, we increase the 'allostatic load' on our bodies resulting in relatively minor illnesses such as heady and body pain and reduced immune resistance.

Sorrow is tied to a loss of something that one was expecting or valued greatly. An extreme case could be the hopelessness or despair one may feel when someone close to him/her dies. At the workplace, sorrow could be about not getting the salary increment, not being able to get through the job interview of a dream company or when a colleague we like working with

---

[1] https://www.prevention.com/life/a20500351/your-body-on-sadness/ (accessed on 22 April 2018).

[2] https://steptohealth.com/happens-brain-depressed/ (accessed on 20 March 2018).

leaves—when a person has hit the wall, and all his/her hopes are dashed.

At the workplace, you would see sad, lonely colleagues, tired of the routine. They make statements such as:

- 'I am so inadequate.'
- 'I won't do well as a manager.'
- 'People will always see me as a weak person.'
- 'The corporate world is a cold, hostile place.'
- 'I have nothing good to offer.'
- 'No one will ever give me a chance again.'

Here are some red flags that might mean you are sorrowful at work:

1. **Impossible to switch off from work**

   Your weekday evenings and weekends are about clearing your mind and switching off. Where is this switch that you can trip and switch off from work?

People in professions that involve emergency services and saving of lives such as the police and doctors can't afford to have that switch; their subconscious is on duty all the time. Are you struggling to find that switch and are unable to stop visualizing what a horrible day you had in office? You don't want to get out of bed the next morning? These are signs of deep sadness at work.

2. **Moan**

If you find yourself moaning all the time about the office, the food they serve, the ways of working, the commute..., these are signs that work is causing sadness in your life. Would you want to be with someone who is always moaning about everything? Imagine having that voice in your head.

Being an introvert is one thing, but avoiding team activities because you hate being around those people is a clear sign of sadness. If you don't enjoy your work, you might not want to interact with your colleagues at social gatherings. If you come to work, avoid lunch in the cafe and are in a rush to leave office, dig deep inside to see if it is down to sorrow you feel at work.

3. **Planned sick leave**

Have you ever planned a sick leave? You wake up on a morning late and instead of gearing up and going to work, you choose to call that you're sick when you are perfectly healthy. And it isn't because you have some other legit reason, it's simply because you don't want to see your workplace—just like a kid who pretends to have a stomach ache to avoid school as they find it a sad place to go to.

4. **The glass is half empty**
   You have had an amazing day in the office. Your manager appreciated you for the work you have done. The senior director has also appreciated you. But you are still thinking about the salary increment you were promised and feel underpaid. Are you looking at reasons why the workplace is at fault no matter what? This is also a sign of work causing sadness.

5. **Health issues**
   Diabetes, high blood pressure, headache and hypertension can all be caused by the workplace too. You cannot keep body out of work. So many executives who have high-flying careers end up with work fatigue at the end of their careers. So many young people develop blood pressure problems because of stress at work. If you are having fatigue or any other health issues apart from checking what you eat, beware of what role your workplace is playing in creating those issues.

6. **Keep snoozing**
   Do you keep hitting the snooze button when it's time to go to work? Do you have multiple alarms set at 6:00 AM, 6:15 AM, 6:30 AM in case you end up cancelling snoozing? Would you do the same if it was you flying out for holidays? Waking up with an alarm is a sign it is time to get ready for work. If you snooze, it shows you are trying to avoid work! And if this is a routine habit, it says a lot about how happy you are in the workplace.

7. **Don't annoy me**
   Do you carry a 'don't mess around with me' tag around the neck or scowl as you peer into a computer

hoping no one will disturb you? Okay, I get it, it's not you; it's your manager. You could have a go at anyone and vent out your steam at small things. It is easy to trigger the hulk in you at the workplace. Or do you carry a cold poker face and no one talks to you as it is? This could be a sign that the workplace makes you sad and you put up an irritated face so that no one messes around and make you feel sadder.

8. **You don't give a damn**
Do you have a long to-do list at work and have excuses for not doing them? Your work is constantly criticized, and you don't really contribute more to keep the salary coming. It is a 'tell' sign. Sometimes you are even ready to get dismissed for bad performance.

9. **Sunday sadness**
On a Sunday, do you start feeling a lump in your throat and a sinking feeling in your chest when you think about having to go to work on Monday? If you just felt it, then you know what this is about. And this is a sign of being sad about the workplace you go.

Seasonal affective disorder (SAD) is worth mentioning here. During winter, when the weather is gloomy or in countries where the weather tends to get too warm, too wet or generally uncomfortable to go around, sick leaves tend to shoot up.[3] This syndrome where a person feels sad because of the low weather is called SAD.

---

[3] https://www.personneltoday.com/hr/help-workers-seasonal-affective-disorder/ (accessed on 20 March 2018).

This disorder is often ignored as an excuse for people not to turn up for work. And any blame on the depressing weather is ignored.

The following are the indications of SAD.

- Low mood
- Feeling tired
- Comfort eating
- Crying outbursts
- Feeling less self-esteem
- General stress levels shoot up

## Chirag's story

2006, New Mumbai.

It was a large call centre like any other in India. And unlike the call centres of the Western world and, increasingly, call centres in India in 2018, there were clear signs that most call centre staff 'wanted' to be there. There wasn't much they could complain about. Call centres were booming in India at the time. The employees were paid well, with a cab to fetch them and drop them home. The air-conditioned office with 24×7 cafés and excellent facilities did everything they could to ensure employee satisfaction. For those fresh out of university and pursuing education externally, it was an awesome work environment. But once monotony kicked in, night shifts became a challenge. There was a girl with this constant mantra during coffee break,

'I have had enough, I am going to resign today.' She had been saying it for almost a year now. Another dude did not care and pretty much sat in his chair taking calls half asleep, and somehow scraped through by barely just achieving targets. There were some who were so down in the dumps that they were forever moaning about cold food in café, difficult targets or how bad the management was and how everything was unfair.

Previously, several of these young people had dreamt of working in an air-conditioned office, with a pick-up and drop facility from office, an office full of fun, a big café and loads of like-minded people to work with. Most important, they were here out of choice. Who would refuse to work in an awesome office and earn as much their parents earned today, right from the beginning of their careers? Chirag was one of these young people, proud of being an earning member of his family.

For Chirag too, initially it was all fun, the thrill of stepping out of the home at night, working with other young people, unlimited coffee, like-minded people, partying hard over the weekend. But once the initial euphoria was over, Chirag used to wake up bleary-eyed, not knowing what time of the day it was.

At first, every call used to be like a surprise package for Chirag. As he told himself, 'You would never know who would call or what they would want. And then you would start getting knocked by people who are angry and swearing at you. Or treat you like dirt and want to speak to a supervisor. Or want to know where you are calling from and then abuse you for the location you are based in. The ring tone which was fun at the beginning, became the alarm for nightmares.

Your body and mind want to run away and hide in a little box.... Your mind is telling you that you want out.'

Chirag was taking more sick leaves and was not able to focus on calls either. He was now put on a performance improvement program (PIP). This was a red flag that meat if you don't improve, you will be shown the exit door. A typical outcome of the PIP (though it is never intended to be so by the company) is that people feel worse about themselves, are often not receptive to the coaching and learning offered during this period, quit on their own or just hang on to the thread till they find another job.

Chirag too was struggling with the bubble he was stuck in, feeling sad to be at work listening to the same ringtone every time the phone rang, every time a customer swore at him. There was only so much his body and mind could take after months of night shifts. Chirag also knew that it was work that he was paid for and he had to perform. His sadness at work and life would not help his circumstances in any way.

Chirag knew he had hit the lowest point in his work, and thus his personal life. But the Chirag inside, the one who had strode into the call centre with hope in eyes, still wanted to be a top performer on the floor. Unfortunately, his supposed 'improvement session' with his floor manager Joe had simply gone downhill with Joe berating the 'likes of him' who were simply not trying hard enough and bringing the floor average and his own performance as a manager down.

Dejected, Chirag walked out of the 'hot room' that his colleagues had nicknamed Joe's cabin and straight to his desk. He typed out a two-line resignation letter and dragged himself to the printer. The printer spewed out his printout. As he bent over to sign the 'nail in the coffin' of his career, a teardrop ruined the wretched piece of paper even further. Frustrated, that even if this was not going right today and that he would have to print again, Chirag turned sharply, swearing under his breath and hitting against something before he passed out for a few seconds.

When he regained consciousness, he was in the 'bedchamber' (another nickname by his colleagues) of the call centre. Peering at him was the nurse on duty Asim and the floor topper Lisa. What was this bugbear Lisa doing here in shift timings? She was the one who supposedly hit sales as if they were ping pong balls. Never took sick leave and was generally the blue-eyed girl of anyone with a 'manager' type of title in the building.

Well, the 'something' Chirag had hit was a box of goodies Lisa had been carrying to distribute among the tiny team she had been assigned to lead during the temporary absence of her boss. But this and other stuff, Chirag got to know later.

First, he had to answer questions on Asim's checklist:

1. 'Are you feeling dizzy Chirag?' No.
2. 'Were you okay when you left home this evening?' Yes.
3. 'Do you have fever, cough, cold, any other illness?' No.
4. 'Would you like water, tea, coffee?' No
5. 'Okay, could you please sign this form to say you are feeling fine now?' Yes.

Your blood pressure, your pulse, everything checked as per the standard operating procedure (SOP) is normal. I think you are good to go home. HR will call you a cab for early departure.

Chirag got up with a start. The 'late mark, the sick leaves, the early departures' all the things against his performance swam before his eyes.

'It's okay Asim'; I'll go back to the floor. I'm okay.'

Chirag got up with a jerk and headed towards the corridor, mulling over whether he should complete his shift and then resign or resign immediately and go home. He knew Joe would accept his resignation within seconds.

Much to his irritation, goody two-shoes Lisa followed him out of the sick room and into the elevator.

'Want to share a milkshake, Chirag, before we go to the floor?' she chirped, smiling her irritating bright smile.

Chirag shook his head and looked away.

Just as they were about to alight on to the fourth floor, Chirag felt it again, the dizziness and was about to sink to the floor. Lisa noticed it too and tightly held on to his arm to steady him. The moment of dizziness passed and they stepped on to the fourth floor.

Lisa announced, 'Juice' and strode towards the cafeteria instead of their desks. Shaken by his spell of dizziness, Chirag followed mutely, dragging his feet.

Having decided she was in charge, Lisa procured a glass of watermelon juice and a banana milkshake and firmly placed the two on one of the tables painted in cheery colours. She waited for Chirag to down the entire glass of watermelon juice at one go. He had just realized how thirsty he was.

'What did you have for dinner Chirag?' she asked.

'No, I didn't like what's on the menu tonight,' he replied.

'Can I ask you for something Chirag?' she asked next.

'No, don't. But I'll answer anyway. I'm on PIP. Everyone is talking about it I know,' Chirag blurted, angry, dejected. He had sensed that some of his colleagues had gossiped that he seemed depressed and needed medication. Others whispered that he was pretending to be sad and was looking for an excuse for not performing well. There were still others who completely avoided conversation with him. They were afraid that if they approached him, he might burst into tears and needed to be left alone.

Lisa took a deep breath and asked firmly,

'That's not what I'm asking Chirag. I was about to ask you if you care for a smoke before we go back to the floor.'

Chirag was taken aback. Though it was common to bond over a smoke, he had never seen Lisa in the smoking zone, at least never during work hours. They walked out to the smoking area.

As Chirag lit up (there was just one left in the packet he was carrying in his pocket), Lisa refused a cigarette. She said she did not smoke or at least not anymore but just wanted to hear Chirag out. She casually remarked that she had been on PIP in her life too—there really was nothing so unique about being on PIP in a call centre or any workplace that was trying to build a performance-oriented culture.

Chirag was shocked. Lisa, who looked as if she was born selling and being the blue-eyed model employee could never have been on PIP!

Lisa had casually asked how many cigarettes he smoked in a day—the answer was something in the range of 18–20. At 5 feet 8 inches, Chirag weighed barely 55 kilos. On the days, he did not like the dinner menu in the cafeteria, he skipped dinner. He refused to carry the dinner his elder sister kindly offered to pack for him. He had tea and a snack before getting into the cab to get to work.

And slowly, everything came pouring out.

Chirag broke down and shared everything at this workplace that made him sad and yet he wanted to stay on. On reflection, Chirag realized that it wasn't just the workplace, but it was certain events in his family life that were making office scenario look worse.

The two made their way to their desks after that watershed conversation, Chirag unsure of success but determined to try and follow the five-point formula Lisa had scribbled on a paper-napkin.

1. Chirag would 'acknowledge' that what he was feeling is deep sorrow, within himself. And his 'customers could hear the sorrow' in his voice too.

2. Chirag would 'analyse' that at least part of the reason for his sorrow was himself, not the nightshift and the evil elements out to get him.

3. Chirag would 'accept' that he needed to change his life himself and not expect his floor manager to get him out of his current state.

4. Chirag would choose his attitude and how he would administer the solution:

   a. Reduce his cigarette consumption by two a day every day for the next 10 days and gradually reach the minimal possible.

   b. Use the mirror given by the team leader to look at himself when he spoke to customers (he had currently stuffed it into his untidy drawer not liking what he was seeing).

   c. Listen to his own calls again with the quality team during break time and listen to their feedback on where and how he could improve.

   d. Consume at least one nutritious meal/a quick snack that he could carry or at least some milkshake instead of surviving on coffee, cigarettes and chocolate.

5. Chirag would act according to his plan and catch up with Lisa for 10 minutes every day to check how he had fared on the four counts.

No surprise really, Chirag was out of PIP in the next 30 days and continues to thrive in the industry.

---

Next time when you go to your workplace, look around carefully. Do you see anyone sad? Any colleague who looks like they are going through a loop of sadness?

Do you see one who is staying to work after 5 PM because they have been told by the manager and they have their kids or a partner waiting at home?

Do you see an average worker being picked on by the manager for every little thing?

Do you see someone being constantly interrupted by somebody else and being told off?

# The Solution Matrix

| Vibhav (Cause) | Sthahi Bhav (Dominant Emotion) | Anubhava (Experience) | Vyabhichari (Related Emotions) | Response |
|---|---|---|---|---|
| Separation from something/ someone you valued | Sorrow | Sadness physically slows down our nervous system, introduces lethargy, fatigue and an urge to cry. We may also have decreased appetite and trouble sleeping; some people experience aches and pains in their body. | Anger, frustration | Less energetic. Often, sadness involves withdrawing from others and becoming quiet and inactive. We may also express our feelings outwardly through crying or sighing. |

## Applying 'A' framework:

| | | |
|---|---|---|
| 1 | Acknowledge | Let yourself know it is okay to be sad. Also, tell yourself that there is no quick way to let it go. Don't be scared and avoid being sad by looking for temporary ways to be happy like retail therapy and doing unwanted shopping. Sadness is a way for your body and mind to let you know there is something wrong. |
| 2 | Analyse | Be curious to find out the root cause of the sadness. Sadness can often be the result of anger that has not turned into sorrow. Feel it deep inside. Do you feel sad in your heart, tummy and shoulders? How is your mind and body feeling? What are the things around you that are triggering the sorrow? What thoughts are making you feel sad? |
| 3 | Accept | Accepting is allowing your emotions to come and go. Feeling it completely and with curiosity, and releasing your emotions. If it's about crying, then do it. Have you ever cried like a baby on your own and felt good? Crying is like a mop-up; it drains out all our negative energy. Crying is a physical activity that helps take the pressure out of the body. The stress hormones are released when we cry. There are other ways to accept sadness. Write your thoughts on a piece of paper. Listen to music that helps you feel deep within your heart. |
| 4 | Administer | Make a list of possible things you can do to deal with the emotion of sadness in the long term. This does not mean getting rid of it; it means having anchors or strategies that will help you manage the emotion better. Try a new thing. Some have been suggested in the following section. But be aware of what you are about to try so you can acknowledge again the impact it has had. |

| 5 | Act | This is doing the hard thing and getting over your sadness. It is the process of knowing how to do it and doing it. As Yoda from *Star Wars* says, 'Do or do not, there is no trying'. It is also about method and discipline—sticking to the action plan you have made, reviewing it regularly and staying away from factors that make you sad. |
| --- | --- | --- |

## Managing Sad Emotions

Following are some tips on how to manage sadness. Try them and list the top three that work for you.

1. **Don't show you are happy if you are not**
   Acceptance is a big step to managing sadness. If you are not happy, don't try and show that you are happy for the sake of it. Focus on doing the minimum work that is required; no one will bother you and allow you to sulk which is okay! When you are feeling that you are at the deepest point in your sorrow, write it down or type it down. Make a list of things bothering you. Don't hold the sad energy in your body; you will pass it around. Find ways to flush it out! Have a change of desk, change the wallpaper on your laptop. Wear something different to the office. Change something, do something different or the same thing differently that would take some of the sadness away.

2. **Watch what you eat**
   The 3-DEM model is all about using science, management and creativity to manage emotions better. Watch what you eat. Cook on your own and eat that which will help increase your energy levels. It will help you manage the phase of sadness better. If given a choice between healthy snacks and a KitKat, don't have a break and eat sugar, eat healthy. That physical energy

will have you be in the game with others and get work done. Occasional desserts are welcome though!

3.  **Carry an emotional care kit**
    Carry in your bag a first-aid kit—a kit to take care of your emotions. For the times when you feel low, you could prepare your personalized toolkit of remedies. For instance, you could have your favourite novel, tea bags or food stored away in your bag, a picture of your favourite people or destination sitting ready in your pocket, or your trusted tablet for a healthy dose of film and television. When you feel sad, you can reach out and do something you like as a part of your break time.

4.  **Desk hibernation**
    If you have absolutely hit the wall and are in no state to come out of it, hibernate at your desk. Make your desk your castle. It's okay to avoid your colleagues for a day and work and eat at your desk. Get snacks at your desk (if allowed at your workplace), finish all work-related things you need and zone out. It will help you dig deep into what is happening in your mind and work on it. Be open to being scared; challenge yourself to be at one place and focus on the work and clear the air that is in your brain. Keep a Rubik's cube or a stress-buster ball at your desk or something to play with when your mind is pacing too fast or too slow.

5.  **Music playlist**
    I know what you are thinking. This is the one every-body is on about. Let's make this a little more interest-ing. Pick a song that you feel like listening to when you are feeling all-time low. Then play it again, and

again till you don't want to listen to it anymore. It helps deep dive into the emotion and detach from it after some time.

6. **Walk**

   Get out of the office to take a walk on your own or with a colleague who understands. Maybe offer this to someone who you can see is going through a sorrow phase. Don't go for a walk during lunch when everyone is out there for their lunch time. Go before or after when it is a little quieter. It is not lunch time, it is walk time. Getting closer to nature will help you freshen up your mind and switch off from work.

7. **Keep away from rotten apples**

   Ever come across people who sound rotten with a standard 'crib list'? You try and share your pain with them, and they make you feel even worse. Keep away from them. Keep the conversation to a minimum and if possible on email, without looking rude. Their chatter will make you worry even more. Connect with the ones who will show you the positive side no matter how low you feel.

8. **30-minute timer**

   Being focused when feeling low is difficult. Keep a timer on your desk and play the 30:5 game. Set a list of tasks, keep track of the watch and complete them in chunks of 30 minutes followed by a five-minute leisure break to access your emotional care kit. This done over a day helps you stay focused on work as you are monitoring your productivity as well as break time closely.

9. **Sit in the washroom**

    Ahem... yes you read it right. Go and rest in the washroom for a while. It is one of the places where you can get some good time by yourself. It is a weird place to introspect in, but it's good to disconnect for a few minutes. Flush out the sorrow from your mind.

Following are the templates you can use to test if you feel sad at work and at what level.

| Question | Never | Occasionally | Sometimes | Most of the Time | All the Time |
|---|---|---|---|---|---|
| Do you feel tired at work? | | | | | |
| Do you feel stressed at work? | | | | | |
| Do you feel uncontrollable stress at the workplace? | | | | | |
| Do you feel hopeless at work? | | | | | |
| Do you feel restless at work? | | | | | |
| Do you struggle to control your restlessness at work? | | | | | |
| Do you feel depressed at work? | | | | | |
| Do you feel everything is a big ask at work? | | | | | |
| Do you feel that you don't understand why everyone is so happy at work, except you? | | | | | |
| Do you feel that you are underemployed at work? | | | | | |
| Total yes | | | | | |

The word 'work' has been used in every question as you need to imagine a scenario of you at your workplace when you select from the options.

Depending on your response, please see in what follows a perspective on what it means:

- **All the time:** You need some help and must speak to one straight away. Seek some help; it is okay!
- **Most of the time:** It will be good to speak to someone, and it is almost the same as all the time.
- **Sometimes:** Assess your career and lifestyle at work and see where you want to improve to manage sadness a little better.
- **Occasionally:** Not saying this is the best block to be in. However, enjoy the drip of sadness work throws at you.
- **Never:** You are a superhero. Share your skills and superpower and how you manage to be sad-proof with the world!

## Question Quotient

When faced with a challenging situation, try and deal with it by working through the following questions:

1. If not reactive, how would you be proactive and deal with sadness before it sinks in?
   This is about catching your thinking and catching the symptom before you acknowledge sadness. Or a part of action could be to see how you will deal with this scenario proactively and play that action in your mind. It will help your mind deal with the scenario better next time.

2. What will your superhero do?

When you are confronted with sorrow and feel like the world is suddenly coming to an end, think about Superman, Batman, Ironman or any other figure you consider a 'superhero'. What would this admirable, inspirational figure do if they were faced with the same hurdles? Think through their response and apply it to yourself.

3. Instead of expecting others to change, what change would you bring to manage this better?

It helps with introspection. What do I need to do with the limited resources I have and what is within my power to change the situation? Do not expect the workplace manager or anyone else to help in the situation. What will you change within you as a starting point?

4. How can you 'serve someone' or yourself powerfully in this time of sadness?

Expand your perspectives and think about what you can do to serve someone or yourself powerfully in this crisis point where you are feeling awfully sad. There are so many people who have a passion or a mission which was the outcome of a sad event they encountered in life—it could be losing someone close or anything else.

5. Do you have any expectations that are not serving you in any way?

You could be sad about many things at the workplace. Can you tell me one expectation that you have that doesn't serve you in any way? An example is expecting a salary increase. It will change when it should. Your moping around will not quicken its pace!

6. How will you learn and grow instead of giving excuses? A way to look at things from a different perspective instead of blaming and coming up with excuses is focussing on how you can learn from the situation.

7. What is your gut telling you?
Listen to your gut. It takes patience and practice, but it does work. Find the answer within you and do what your instinct tells you to.

8. What is the first step you can take to allow happiness to come in?
It is a perfect question to figure out how to put away the blame and look for something that can make you smile. Don't focus on too many perspectives or analyses, just the first tiny action that will make you smile. A small breakthrough will have a big impact.

9. If being good was the answer to be less sad, what is good enough for you?
Do not seek perfection in everything. Don't look to be the greatest and the best. Being good enough is not seeking perfection but being content with the minimum you get.

10. Will this thing that is making me sad matter to me in a months' time, in a years' time and in 10 years?
We get trapped in the present and become sad when something doesn't happen. Sometimes when we look back at our lives, we realize the bad times were the best things that ever happened to us. Similarly, fast-forward the sad moment you are in and see when it will stop mattering. Once you see it, then it won't really matter—sadness vanishes.

11. Who do you need to be to become what you want to be?

    You are feeling sad, and you are feeling low. Once you know how you would like to feel, what do you have to become to be that person? Dressing smart might help you change your mindset. Eating healthy might give you some more confidence.

Peace

*Peace cannot be kept by force; it can only be achieved by understanding.*

—Albert Einstein

# The Manifestation of Peace at the Workplace

The survey revealed the following results. Out of the individuals surveyed,

- Over 94 per cent felt strong emotions while at work, whether they were related to work or not.
- 52 per cent had trouble managing their emotions while at work.
- 35 per cent left a job due to feeling strong emotions or struggling to manage emotions.
- Among the emotions that respondents were struggling to manage at the workplace before they moved away from jobs were: 43 per cent said anger, 30 per cent said disgust, 13 per cent said fear.
- 77 per cent said their workplace would benefit from new or improved support and resources for dealing with strong emotions while at work.
- 64 per cent used or leveraged emotions to improve productivity.
- 67 per cent have successfully used peace/calm to improve the pace or quality of their work.

## Depicting 'Peace' in the Arts

In the traditional depictions of peace/calm in dance or drama, the protagonist is in a meditative pose, the eyes either closed or looking far into the horizon absorbed in a vision that sometimes only they can see. The body language depicts a state that is higher than the state of achievement (seen in wonder or heroism). It depicts harmony of the body and mind, cohesion or settling down of the erstwhile fighting forces by having achieved the zenith that one yearns for but does not find possible to achieve during the active play of the other eight emotions.

While in Greek mythology, the goal is achievement (Hercules climbing the mountain), in Hindu philosophy, the goal is inner peace (Pattnaik 2016). But often, in Eastern and Western cultures, heroism and resultant wonder are the prerogatives of the heroes and heroines engaging in active combat to make the world a better place. Meanwhile, the peace that one sees in the arts is rarely found in the eyes of the active ruler. It is more likely to be seen in the eyes of the older, wiser, former protagonist who has voluntarily renounced the pursuit of achievement and fame. These are therefore individuals who have re-defined what achievement means to them.

The subtle difference that is of prime importance is studying the body language of one who has vanquished an external enemy (the hero that inspired wonder in many) and the one who has gained control over his own emotion and ability to vanquish the 'internal enemy'. This is the hero/heroine who has 'been there, done that!' and is rarely thus perturbed by the wild vagaries of the world of work.

## 'Peace' in Science

Stress, as we know, causes the 'fight or flight' response. The body prepares its defence against stress through physiological and behavioural adaptations. Stress hormones flood our system and can really help us overcome an emergency. In the long term, we do not need these at all as they can lead to chronic conditions.

Oxytocin is the hormone effective in producing anti-stress effects. The release of oxytocin occurs during lactation in new mothers. It is also released in the presence of positive relationships, social contact and networks (Uvnäs-Moberg 1997, 38–42). Negative stress need not always be due to an external situation but could also be due to 'internal events' such as thoughts, feelings and habitual behaviours.

This is regarding 'distress' or bad stress that causes anxiety, decreases performance and could lead to mental and physical problems. However, not all stress is bad. In fact, the complete absence of stress could lead to extreme complacence or inertia, not recommended at any workplace.

'Eustress', or positive stress is usually within our coping abilities, is short-term, generates a feeling of excitement and helps us focus our energy and improve performance.

However, it is possible that what an individual perceives as eustress is seen as distress by another. For example, some people perceive change as opportunity, while for others it can cause extreme negative stress. This is dependent on a variety of factors including one's experience with these changing situations, their ability to cope with the change or their natural tendency.

# Experiencing peace at the workplace— Yasu's story

March 2015, Bangalore, India.

With the remnants of confetti still stuck on the back of his Armani jacket and the sweet sound of the cheers echoing, Yasu stepped out of Trident Corporation for the last time. After a decade-plus in the corporation and the goodwill he had nurtured and helped build, his core team had organized a spectacular farewell event. He had been deeply touched, but had refused to shed a tear—at least in public. It had been a brilliant run and he certainly had more great memories than regrets. One of his regrets, though, was Yatin.

But before we move to Yatin, let's talk about Yasu.

'Yasu'—what was that? Why would anybody grant such a random name to their child way back in the 1950s when standard God names were in vogue in India and exotic 'global' baby names had still not made an appearance as a fashion statement?

Whenever anyone asked him what that meant, pat came Yasu's answer, 'From the Japanese 安 (Yasu) means peace, quiet', 康 (Yasu) meaning 'peaceful' or 坦 (Yasu) meaning 'flat, smooth, level'. And then he would quip, the pace of his speech often too rapid for listeners to grasp what he was saying:

'Doesn't sound like me, right? Maybe it was just wishful thinking by my late father imposing his "international outlook" on my poor mother! My mother, my wife, my children, my bosses, my colleagues— everyone seems to agree on one thing, if something was needed yesterday, I'd probably have done it the day before! And if anyone tried to do it any later than today, well, Yasu's wrath knew no bounds. And even worse for the person, he/she would find that it was already half done.'

May 2004, flashback to Bangalore, India.

In his board meetings, reviews with his senior leaders and the 'war rooms' created to handle 'human-generated corporate disasters', Yasu would term this as the 'cost of leadership'— 'What you had to pay to be a leader and to achieve what you set out to. The "payment" would include deep commitment to your cause with sleep deprivation, biologically challenging stretches of work hours and schedules that would challenge your physical and mental health.'

When these words were uttered, they received a variety of responses. Those who wanted to join the boys at the pub to watch that crucial game gritted their teeth and swore under their breath for Yasu's invasion into their space demanded by 'work life balance'.

Still others would look at Yasu intently, the eyes focused on the strategy he had outlined on the whiteboard, pretend to take notes, all the while intent on working with the person seated across the table to 'not' make it happen! And when Yasu bellowed in the next review why it had not happened, the answers were ready— fluctuations in the market, the response time of the customer or flaws in Yasu's strategy in the first place.

And those who looked up to Yasu as the person who would help them succeed, nodded and smiled in agreement, once more determined to walk the path he would set out and 'make things happen'.

Among these people was Yatin, a young graduate who had joined Yasu's team as a junior manager in sales. Unlike the polished bunch of MBAs in finely crafted shirts and silk ties, Yatin stood out with his tacky embroidered shirts, slightly comical moustache and gruff demeanour. Like he often did, Yasu had spotted something special in the youngster for the one thing his peers struggled to do, primarily due to the jargon they spouted before unsuspecting and thus cynical customers but Yatin seemed to achieve customer trust naturally. He simply told customers what they were buying, using a mix of the three languages spoken in Bangalore—English, Kannada and Hindi. Yatin was terrible at all three, hailing from a grocer's family in Gujarat. But the good news was, the customers were not great at English either, their source of Hindi was Bollywood (the same as Yatin's) and they deeply appreciated Yatin's attempt to pick up the appropriate operative words in their native Kannada. Most important, they liked Yatin's curious mix of earnest sales and willingness to please without the attempt (and honestly the ability) to please them with a swanky presentation.

In the same way, Yasu had observed that Yatin rarely took notes during Yasu's exhortations to the team to run faster than the wind. But Yasu had observed that ultimately Yatin seemed to accomplish what Yasu wanted. But whatever Yatin accomplished, it was never enough for Yasu. From reprimanding Yatin for his grammatical errors, for not polishing his shoes and stubble to pushing him to the limit in building a diverse team, Yatin bore the brunt of Yasu's short temper.

Over the next five years, Yatin gradually shed his 'Yatinisms', pushed himself to attend short courses at the top management institute Yasu recommended and slowly began to step out of his comfort zone.

April 2013.

Yasu announced his decision to retire in the next two years. As the hotly debated search for his successor gathered momentum, Yatin was soon emerging as a likely candidate. Over the years, he had borne the 'cost of leadership' and his contribution to Trident was well known across customer segments and markets. Yasu prepared to establish his legacy, closing deals, consolidating existing customer relationships, creating history for Trident.

With the same fervour, he employed his strength behind Yatin's candidature. As the lobbying continued, so did the final pieces of Yatin's top management coaching. The 'CEO circle' that Yasu propagated had been completed by Yatin in his tenure so far. On his own accord and the rest on Yasu's goading, Yatin had completed stints in different parts of the company, some he enjoyed, others he was petrified of attempting and still others he managed to scrape through but learnt on the job. The final pieces were more to do with chiselling away the rough edges of an already-polished statue!

Back to March 2015, Bangalore, India.

When the board announced Trident's new Chief Executive, a gentleman who had recently relocated to India from the UK, Yatin had been deeply disappointed; and Yasu? Strangely, for someone who usually flung his feelings across to his teams and the war rooms reverberated with the roar, it was difficult to decipher what Yasu really felt.

March 2017, Chennai.

For the first time in 12 years, Yasu and Yatin had not interacted for two years. Though the other had forgotten him, neither passed a week without thinking of each other and of the Trident they had built together. And yet, the phone call, the visit that should have taken place or just a text message or quick email, never did.

Under the shadow of doubt that his allegiance to his mentor was the sole reason that he was not picked for the top position, or worse, that his mentor really did not pitch enough for him after all...Yatin exited from Trident. After a struggle with two start-ups for a few months, he bagged an assignment with a large corporation based in the Middle East.

Soon after his departure from Trident and having 'been there, done that', Yasu had partnered with a younger industry management expert to launch a 'finishing school' to groom chief executives for the industry.

As an entrepreneur, the pressure to pay salaries, rents and make profits every quarter was higher than ever before and Yasu's boardroom resembled a war room again. Time sped by again. But this time, Yasu's battle was less within and more a screenplay designed to help his younger partner carry forward a profitable business without him. As they designed budgets and targets for the year ahead, once again under pressure to meet numbers, Yasu said something which would have shocked his colleagues at Trident:

'I want people to feel happy they have achieved something and go home satisfied, otherwise, you are always cutting things too fine—leave the margin you need in your targets, budgets, costs and most important—your time.'

Diagnosed with an incurable form of cancer, his health deteriorated, not by the long hours in the boardroom and crazy travel but by chemotherapy. Yasu spent his last six months in and out of hospital. He discouraged people to visit him in hospital but in the 'good weeks in between', he continued to coach senior executives, conduct management training and proffer advice over breakfast to the likes of those who wanted to follow the path he chalked out during his 'war room days'.

During one such breakfast session, Yasu had a surprise participant. During a brief India trip, Yatin flew down to Chennai to catch Yasu's advice over breakfast. In a relatively small group of senior executives seated around the horse-shoe shaped table, Yasu spotted Yatin in just a few seconds. He nodded at him and continued his discourse,

'At the workplace, surround yourself with people who want to go with you. If you don't have people who want to go with you and the battlefield is agog, place your finger on the pulse of your troops. If the direction of their work is not focused towards a customer/enemy or an external force you aim to satisfy, there is a strong danger of them killing each other. All you will have is blood on the battlefield. Do you know what happened to the Yadavas (Krishna's clan) in the great ancient Indian epic Mahabharata? They had the curse of the deeply hurt and angry "self-blinded Queen Gandhari" that unleashed the "enemy within". Even when the great warrior Arjun was dispatched to save the Yadavas who remained and bring back the survivors of his mentor Krishna's clan, he came back empty handed. Well, no-one had survived!'

As the motley gathering of CEOs in the making split into groups debating what was more dangerous for performance management—disloyalty or incompetence—and whether they should tolerate either, both or neither, Yasu sunk into his seat at the head of the table.

Yatin cast a furtive glance at him and noticed how gradual this action of settling into his chair had been. Usually a master at group discussions and proactive in offering to present, Yatin fell silent, waiting for the session to get over, with apprehension and regret. That was what had dragged Yatin here today.

After his exit from Trident 'under a cloud' as the gossip mill churned, Yatin had cut off contact with most people he knew at Trident. The peer groups that had ridiculed him in his early years had had no choice but to respect the position he had attained in the end, but most of them had done that with the selfish motive of plain survival—what if Yatin became the CEO of Trident? They needed their jobs and plum positions in the management teams. As soon as Yatin exited and the new CEO stepped in, the thrones had inched closer to the new boss from the UK. Others in the rest of the organization simply refrained from reaching out—for no specific reason. Of course, Yatin had a few of his supporters, but he refused to respond to their attempts to reach out.

And then, given the furious outbreak of social media groups, someone had added Yatin to the Trident Alumni social group. Still seething under what Trident took away from him, Yatin was about to exit the group when he chanced upon a message about Yasu's health that left him sweating—even in the artificial cold of the super air conditioning to beat the dry and hot Dubai air.

The breakfast session was over; the participants exited slowly, a lady sharing cards with Yasu, one asking when his next session would be, another checking if Yasu would be available to speak on a panel in Mumbai in the next quarter.

'Sure, please do get in touch closer to the date,' Yasu smiled at the gentleman, still seated. Finally, when the room was empty, Yatin mustered the courage to walk up to Yasu. The master salesman and now the CEO of a mid-sized company, Yatin was tongue-tied. He was still reeling under the shock of seeing the deep dark circles under Yasu's eyes, the hair that he had lost and for the first time in 12 years—Yatin was seeing Yasu in a business environment without his signature three-piece suit but dressed in a simple linen shirt and grey trousers!

But Yatin did not have to say anything or even extend his hand. Once again, Yasu was in charge. As if nothing had changed, but because everything had, he said,

'Yatin, give me your hand. I will need help to stand up. I've lost 22 kilos over the past few months.'

Yatin mutely extended his hand, tears welling up. As the two walked down the staircase, Yasu holding on to Yatin's elbow for support, Yatin's tears continued to flow freely. Once again, as if nothing had changed and because everything had, Yasu continued his barrage of usual questions to Yatin,

'So, what are you doing now? Who are the investors in this company? Oh, I know someone on the board of one of their close competitors. Do you have a team you trust?' Yatin answered these dutifully. And as was their ritual, presented Yasu with his latest business card.

Yasu peered into the embossed lettering, 'I need to go into the next session Yatin and will need to rest after that. But I'm very proud, my boy! Can I still call you that?'

Yatin finally smiled through his tears and asked, 'Yasu, how can I leave without a nugget of advice per meeting?'

Yasu smiled broadly and this is how he ended the last ever meeting with his mentee:

'If you want to achieve the impossible in an active leader's life, you will continue to bear the cost of leadership and you should! You have miles to go; there is no room or time for complacence. But I will now tell you what I have never told you before. It is not that I held it back. But I had not experienced this before.

What I taught you over the years was rarely from a management theory book, but simply what I learnt when I thrashed about for survival and after a strong swim across the corporate ocean. But during the past two years and especially the last six months, I have experienced this and wished someone had told this to me earlier:

As you pay the cost of leadership and lead with passion, you will experience extreme negative emotions—"fear" of failure, "anger" at those who attack you, "sorrow" for those who let you down, "disgust" for the depths of corporate politics. You will also experience more exhilarating highs, "love" for the people who support you and work chemistry with the ones who you choose to run the marathon with, "heroism" when you overcome the obstacles and "wonder" at success that you never imagined will be yours.

*Remember to demonstrate the emotional elasticity to be drawn into these wondrous emotional moods for they make work life worth it, not the numbers that die with the people who achieve them.* But even as you experience these highs and lows through emotional elasticity, do not let any of these touch your core. The resonance you seek should be with the unshaven Yatin who walked into the board meeting years ago, wearing an embroidered shirt and dusty sandals but with his heart in the work he was doing, his soul in the impossible he was to achieve. That is the Yatin you will take home with you, not the companions who generate and often share the emotional moods that you experience. Keep the curse of the Blind Queen of success and fame away from your soul—love your work, not your job. While you still retain the fire in your (now bulging) belly (he smiled broadly), do not ruin your sleep or the time that rightfully belongs to your loved ones with strife. Watch the dance of the *Navarasas* at work as if it is a drama unfolding on screen. Play your part and step out when you need to.

At least once a day, do what makes you "smile"—for no apparent reason! Play with your dog or a child, run, swim, catch a glimpse of your favourite person, picture, cause or anything else.... May peace be with you!'

# The Solution Matrix—3-DEM Applied to Peace

As we established, the answer to managing emotion lies in the confluence of the three: (a) the arts (b) management science (c) medical science.

## Building the 3-DEM Action Plan: Establishing Peace at the Workplace

In the case of Yasu, as per the *Navrasa* theory, the state of the *rasa* manifests due to the cause or trigger of the emotion (*vibhav*), the effect of the emotion is the *anubhava* and the transient/related emotions are the *vyabhichari*. While *rasas* denote the mood, these *bhavas* (associated with each *rasa*) create the mood through physical media—the brain, body or action.

Table 11.1, based on the arts, helps us classify the emotions connected with the dominant emotion of peace.

**Table 11.1**  Emotions Connected with the Dominant Mood of Peace

| Vibhav (Cause) | Sthahi Bhav (Dominant Emotion) | Anubhava (Experience) | Vyabhichari (Related Emotions) | Response | | |
|---|---|---|---|---|---|---|
| | Shanta Rasa | | | Uttama (high) | Madhyama (medium) | Adhama (low) |
| Arrival of a solution to a problem or having accepted that one needs to achieve peace despite the existence of the problem | Peace | Calm, balance, no turmoil, no discord | Satisfaction, slight apathy | Inspiration for others, no negative response even in the face of severe provocation | Moderate energy, activity | Inertia, laziness |

The aim is to achieve the balance among positive and negative emotions—the anti-fragile being the zenith of emotion—peace (Figures 11.1–11.4).

**Figure 11.1**  The Anti-fragile and Peace

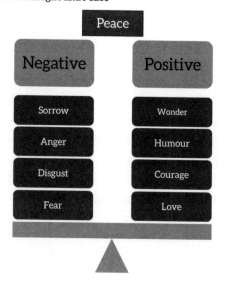

**Figure 11.2** Analysing the Negative Emotional Moods

**Figure 11.3** Analysing the Positive Emotional Moods

**Figure 11.4** Planning for Peace

How can you apply the 5A framework?

How could Yasu have established peace? The answer is by applying the 5As framework.

| 1 | Acknowledge | This situation needs me to rise above the ordinary and still take care of myself. | Having experienced intense activity to 'get the job done' at the workplace and multiple forces driving the destabilization of my mind and peace, I need to take care of myself. |
|---|---|---|---|
| 2 | Analyse | I must put into categories what I'm really feeling (among the nine emotions) and understand at least some of what happens in the brain. | Based on what I have categorized, I will be able draw an action plan towards achieving the anti-fragile. |
| 3 | Accept | Peace is preceded by turmoil, intense activity. | During the course of my work, I journey through all of the eight emotional moods, I'm elated, I'm involved, I am awestruck, I'm afraid, I'm sad, I'm angry, I'm disgusted. There is no automatic peace at the workplace. I need to work towards achieving it. |
| 4 | Administer | I will 'choose' my attitude. | I need to build inner strength where my core remains intact even in the face of severe provocation, fire-fighting, turmoil. |
| 5 | Act | I will 'follow' my plan. | When situations leading to any of the negative emotions attack, I need to take them on board, analyse the sources threadbare and temper them with positive emotions so that every day I work, I will be closer to my intended state of peace. |

# References

Pattanaik, Devdutt. 2016, October 17. *Olympus* (Paperback). New Delhi: Penguin Books.

Uvnäs-Moberg, K. 1997. 'Oxytocin Linked Antistress Effects—The Relaxation and Growth Response.' *Acta Physiologica Scandinavica Supplement* 640: 38–42. Review.

CHAPTER

# 12

# Conclusion: The Journey Towards the Anti-fragile

Who doesn't welcome a positive emotional mood? Delight, humour, love, wondrous situations and demonstrations of courage at the workplace are a pleasure to witness and experience. The lessons from these four positive moods are on how one can leverage these to enhance one's own and other people's performance at the workplace.

Naturally, all of these need to be used in moderation in order to be effective. Too much fun or camaraderie at the workplace could end up diluting the seriousness and focus that good performance requires. Also, courage needs a break! Situations that incessantly demand the demonstration of courage could end up burning out people.

We have seen the negative impact of extreme emotional moods through the case studies—sadness at being let down, anger at being cheated, fear of losing what you treasure and disgust leading to revulsion against the situation itself. The short-term outcome of each of the four negative moods would lead to the obvious detriments—loss of motivation, productivity, sustained negativity, tendency to give up and more.

Each of us in our personal and work lives would have suffered from the ill-effects of at least one of (if not all) the four emotional moods. The most important aspect is how the situations leading to these moods were handled and what one did or others did to help overcome these negative emotional moods. The most obvious and often applied solution is to get out of the situation itself—separate oneself from the work/job that has generated such extreme emotional moods.

Whether it is a case of bullying, provocation, victimization, case building as a political agenda or whatever else, the person who is at the receiving end needs to first stand up and ask himself whether it is worth remaining in the situation. If the conclusion is that the situation is far too difficult/uncomfortable to remain in and if there is a choice, the first step towards recovery would be moving on.

There really is no right or wrong answer to whether one should stick on or not as it is dependent on individual preferences, importance given to work, tolerance levels and what each one's purpose in life is.

Whatever the reason for sticking on, financial dependence on the workplace, lack of other options or the desire to win, the true test of resilience is the ability of a person to live through this trial by fire.

When people decide to stick on, despite situations and people leading to adverse emotional moods, they have just accelerated their learning. At every juncture of their trial period, these people are learning something new—how deception occurs at the workplace, how one cannot always control everything, how situations arise with no logical explanation on why, how bad things can get and, most important, what one can do to overcome them. With every blow they deal with, they convert a 'black swan' into a 'grey swan' with a much better idea of how they should deal with the next time they may encounter a similar situation.

Even as they experience trials and tribulations and sometimes flounder, at other times deal with them with courage, they need to learn that however intense the situation, the ultimate journey should be towards maintaining inner peace—placing a screen between yourself and the unfolding scene.

And this is really the journey towards making oneself stronger, the journey towards the 'anti-fragile'.

# About the Authors

**Manjiri Gokhle Joshi** is CEO, Global Talent Track (GTT), a company specializing in training and CSR projects, with the mission to make India employable.

She has a master's degree in Mega-Project Management from Said Business School, University of Oxford. Prior to this, Manjiri and her husband Abhay Joshi co-founded Elephant Connect, helping students and professionals transform their lives through school and university education and leadership training.

In 2016, Manjiri was one of the 12 professionals among 13,000 applicants selected by LinkedIn and Virgin Media to assist Virgin Founder Richard Branson judge, select and mentor entrepreneurs for a UK-wide contest for a 1-million-pound fund across the UK.

In 2009, she co-founded Maya CARE, a charity, working with senior citizens. She is a recipient of the British High Commission Chevening Scholarship (2006).

She has authored four other books: *Inspired*, lessons from 23 contemporary inspirational leaders (co-author Dr Ganesh Natarajan), 2006; *Crushes, Careers and Cell Phones*, Foreword by former Miss Universe Sushmita Sen, 2011; *Bosses of the Wild: Lessons from the Corporate Jungle*, Foreword by Mr K.V. Kamath, Chairman, ICICI Bank, 2013 and *Maya*, Foreword by Shabana Azmi, 2016. Among her past assignments are Learning and Development Specialist and Head, Project Management (Primal) at Informa PLC, London; Programme Manager, GlobalLogic, UK; National Management and Head, Corporate Communication, ICICI Lombard, Mumbai; Head, Contact Centre and Head, Human Resources, Zensar BPO;

Assistant Editor, Dataquest, New Delhi and a reporter with the *Indian Express*.

**Manjeet Singh** has over decade of project consulting experience with brands such as Zensar Technologies, Marks & Spencer, Amazon, Harvey Nichols, Debenhams and Burberry in London. Founder of Yoviva Ltd, his vision is to help people transform their mindset to play beyond their comfort zone through coaching. Manjeet has a master's degree in business from Pune University and holds an associate coach certification from International Coach Federation. Manjeet started his professional career working in a call centre during his university days, where he was introduced to the world of selling and coaching.

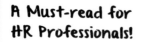